Dale Morrison's story reminds us that life with cancer or adversity of any kind requires resiliency and perseverance. Each page of *Hope and Help from a Cancer Survivor* tells a narrative of faith, hope, and love that will provide encouragement and inspiration to the countless individuals enduring the extra mile of cancer.

Roger Staubach
Dallas Cowboys' Hall of Fame Quarterback

I am a scientist, and as such, I have been trained to look for logical, science-based explanations for events. And yet, I am mindful of Dale's enormous faith in God that incorporates a fervent prayer life that seeks God's guidance, healing, and answers to tribulations and trials. I know that Dale and his family and friends have approached God through prayerful petition on his behalf, asking for victory over his illness. It is evident that they give God the credit for his recovery, whether it was miraculous or brought about by the wisdom bestowed by God upon Dale's treating physicians. Regardless of one's belief, we can all be encouraged that science and faith meshed together to result in a healthy man who overcame dismal and bleak odds to regain his health and vitality. For that, we can all agree: "This was a miracle."

J. Donald Capra, MD
The late President Emeritus of the Oklahoma Medical Research Foundation who died from a malignant brain tumor, known as glioblastoma multiforme, in February 2015

Dale Morrison has written a compelling journal of his ministry, his faith in God, and his journey from advanced cancer to wholeness and health. With God, modern medicine, and nutrition as his synergistic therapies (in that order), Dale has given the reader a modern translation of the Scriptural passage Psalm 23:4: *Even when I walk through the darkest valley, I will not be afraid, for you are close beside me. Your rod and your staff protect and comfort me.* Excellent book for those battling some severe disease.

Patrick Quillin, PhD, RD, CNS
Author of *Beating Cancer With Nutrition*

Dale remained positive despite his understandable fears of the unknown. He was accepting of what might come, but was not passive in his approach to health. He was a person in need, but recognized opportunities for giving. As he improved, he turned his sights toward helping others going through this difficult journey. He has been an inspiration not just to other patients, but also to our care team. Dale beat the odds, but in some ways, I am not surprised. If anyone could do it, Dale could.

Benjamin Greenberg, MD
Associate Professor at UT Southwestern Medical Center

Ike Eisenhower had his General Patton; Tom Landry had his Roger Staubach; and the good Lord has His Dale Morrison. *Hope and Help* is the story of a faith in God that refuses to cave in or give up even when life's battles appear to be unwinnable. Virtually every page of Dale's remarkable story underscores the words of the apostle Paul: *We are troubled on every side, yet not distressed; … afflicted in every way, but not crushed; … we are perplexed, but not in despair; … cast down, but not destroyed; … in all these things we are more than conquerors through him that loved us.*

Reverend Stan Allcorn
Pastor, Pioneer Drive Baptist Church, Abilene, Texas

Dale's candid and emotional journey gives readers a unique window into the heart of a man willing to bare his soul so that others may themselves find hope and help. Faith, family, and fortitude are what helped Dale throughout his diagnosis and recovery. In this book, he coaches readers to fight the good fight and win whatever battle they may be facing.

Aaron R. Baggett, Ph.D.
Assistant Professor, Department of Psychology,
University of Mary Hardin-Baylor

Hope and Help

from a

Cancer Survivor

Hope and Help

from a

Cancer Survivor

A Memoir of Faith Amidst Affliction

Dale Morrison
with Jacob West

Visit Dale's website: www.hopeandhelp.net

Hope and Help from a Cancer Survivor – Dale Morrison, With Jacob West

Copyright © 2015

First edition published 2015

Scripture quotations are taken from the 1611 Authorized King James Bible.

Cover Design: Amber Burger

Cover Photography: comussu/Shutterstock

Editors: Gloria Graham, Donna Sundblad, RuthZetek

Printed in the United States of America

Aneko Press – *Our Readers Matter*™

www.anekopress.com

Aneko Press, Life Sentence Publishing, and our logos are trademarks of

Life Sentence Publishing, Inc.

203 E. Birch Street

P.O. Box 652

Abbotsford, WI 54405

BIOGRAPHY & AUTOBIOGRAPHY / Religious

Paperback ISBN: 978-1-62245-294-1

eBook ISBN: 978-1-62245-295-8

10 9 8 7 6 5 4 3 2 1

Available where books are sold.

Share this book on Facebook:

CONTENTS

FOREWORD

By Robert Collins, M.D.
Director of Hematologic Malignancies/
Blood and Marrow Transplantation Program
University of Texas Southwestern Medical Center

I'm very grateful that I've been able to get to know Dale so well as his doctor, although I'm sure we both wish we could have met some other way!

From the day we first met, I was struck by his strength and matter-of-fact courage, his concern for others even while he was in the thick of his own battles, and most of all, of course, his deep and very apparent faith.

Dale is very out-front with his faith – there's no question where he stands. Moreover, it is very clear his faith is the bedrock on which everything else in his life stands.

When we first met, he was just an unbelievably great guy. I remember at one point we had to get going with his treatment (we didn't really have a lot of time to spare), but he insisted on going to Haiti first to help earthquake victims. A quiet "wow" was the response from all of us taking care of him.

From the very beginning, he was always reaching out to other patients in our clinic and helping them however he could. Whether it was advice on diet, or prayer, or dealing with a new diagnosis, he was always there for them. I've so often, over the years, heard from one patient or another: "Yeah, I met this guy in the waiting room, and he was so helpful to me and my wife.

He said just the right thing. I forget his name." I'd say, "Dale, right?" And they'd say, "Yeah, that's it. Dale!" And I've more than once sent patients specifically his way because I was trying to encourage them, and I knew that only another patient who had been in the same place would really be able to help. And Dale did help them.

As solid as Dale is, though, he's the first to tell you that he was a long way from where he ought to be, where he's meant to be. And he tells you that his illness has been an occasion of real growth for him, in faith, trust, and love. He managed to hang on, to stay faithful through it all. And he was wrapped up in the prayers of probably thousands. So much trust, such complete dependence on higher things. In that setting, God moved to help Dale grow closer to Himself.

Just like Dale will tell you, he's grown in this process, and others have too. This book looks back over this whole process, this long story of Dale's ordeal, and all the people affected by it in addition to him. This includes family, friends, doctors, nurses, other healthcare workers, and so many others – some close, and some far, far away, but all were touched in some way.

So many stories from Dale's odyssey – so many ways to glimpse good coming out of all the bad. Certainly new medical insights have developed that we are able to use for others, as well as countless stories of other people helped in one way or another as God brought good out of the whole thing. And I know too that my faith was deepened in a way that has helped me to become a better doctor – more of a healer, in the fuller sense of the word – for my patients.

At times, God allowed me to see pretty clearly how lives were affected in a good way, despite all the dire circumstances and all the suffering Dale went through. But beyond what I could see, I know too that others were affected subtly. Some saw clearly because their lives were affected in a beautiful way, and many others managed to get a glimpse and perceive it from God's view.

A great Christian writer and mystic, Simone Weil, once wrote: "The extreme greatness of Christianity lies in the fact that it does not seek a supernatural remedy for suffering, but a supernatural use for it." And that's the point. God doesn't fix everything. Even if Dale is better now, something else may come up one of these days to get the better of him, hopefully not for a long, long time, however. But, as the saying goes, none of us gets out of this thing alive.

I'd say that my faith has been deepened by the whole process of taking care of Dale, of knowing him and his family, and of seeing things play out. I'll say that at the time I met Dale a few years ago, faith was a strong part of my life as well. It's a long story, but just suffice it to say that I used to be very much an agnostic, until God's grace really began to move in my life. This was done through a few flashes of insight here and there, some really great authors, and, without question, a number of very faithful patients who were able to bring me along by their kindness, their love, and their example of quiet faith and trust even in the worst of times. So when I met Dale and his family, I was very much a believer too, and I understood where Dale was coming from. I so appreciated his praying for me and my colleagues, and I prayed for him too.

In the time I've known Dale, my faith has grown in a very real and important way. I've come to appreciate that when a person's faith is growing, it's because of a *wave* of God's grace. How grateful we can be! And this is my experience – that in some way, Dale's deep faith and trust in the midst of his trial played a role in deepening my faith. Ultimately, it's very mysterious how this stuff works, isn't it? "If you understand it, it's not God," goes one saying. We can be grateful for the gift of God's grace, and we can be grateful for those whom God uses to help bring the gift to us in some way. And I'm grateful for Dale.

ACKNOWLEDGMENTS

I am so thankful for the Heavenly Father who gave me this life with my family and friends, and heard our prayers and saw our tears; for the Savior who died for the atonement of my sin, and for the Holy Ghost who sustains me.

I have nothing but my deepest love and gratitude for my wife, Nancy, for the way she has patiently cared for me over the last decade and has sincerely loved me all these years. She is my hero.

I also appreciate the encouragement Jacob West offered by writing my story and for believing that it was a story that others would want to read.

INTRODUCTION

I magine the darkest night. How long would it last? How void would the sky seem of stars and the moon? How long would the sun delay its rising? Nights on childhood camp-outs felt as if the night resisted the sun's rising. I looked out the screened-in porch – what seemed like every hour –looking for daylight. As much as I enjoyed the adventure of camping out, building fires, and running through the pasture, the long night with its eerie sounds reinforced that home was far away. Howls from coyotes mingled with owls hooting to claim their territory, and these joined the mechanical thumping of an oilfield pumpjack. These once-scary sounds heard as a child while at my family's farm in Malakoff, Texas, are now comforting tones.

I write the following story to tell of a long night spent in physical pain, loneliness, uncertainty, and confusion. However, through every night, my family and I always knew the joy of the morning light would soon come. My conviction came from God's Word. I read repeatedly in Proverbs to trust God completely and that He would direct my path. The proverb reads, *Trust in the Lord with all thine heart; and lean not unto thine own understanding. In all your ways acknowledge him, and he shall direct they paths.* The passage became a life verse I shared with others and used to guard against fear. The treatments had to end, the scared frown on a child's face had to relax, and the promise of God's faithfulness would be evident.

I am the elder son to Dale and Delores Morrison. I am

Nancy's husband. Courtney, Emily, and Malory call me Daddy. Carson, Callie, Ellie, Ryan, Addison, Andrew, Natalie, Corley, and Brooklyn call me Coach instead of Grandpa. Many know me as friend, businessman, mentor, and life encourager.

Anyone familiar with my story knows me as a man who has endured and won victories of the variety that leave seasoned doctors in awe. And for those who love me dearly, my story leaves them thanking God for one more miracle when I had already received my fair share of divine intervention.

This story shares how God creates every person for a specific task and purpose. God gives us a free will to choose the best path. For me, the best path is where my intentions, ideas, and activities align with God's plan. In other words, I want to walk on God's path. It's far superior to anything I can construct.

My belief system includes the notion that God sometimes takes a person down a hard road in order to encourage others or to learn an important lesson that we wouldn't get if life were smooth and convenient. This story weaves together my battle with non-Hodgkin's lymphoma, an attack on my central nervous system called progressive multifocal leukoencephalopathy/JC virus, my first granddaughter's brain tumor, and my bone marrow transplant. All the while, the family's collective faith in God, strong friendships, and the Lord's use of groundbreaking science made a substantial difference in my life and in potentially thousands of others' lives in the future.

1

MUSTARD SEED, MEET
THE MOUNTAIN

Our vehicle settled into traffic at a high point in Port-au-Prince, the broken capital of a desperate nation. A little over a week earlier, an earthquake had brought this proud western half of the island to its knees. In every direction, I saw toppled buildings, strands of rebar, and strewn pieces of roadway. The sirens blared constantly, as if we might forget someone was in need. Along with the devastation, desperation had invaded the western half of Hispaniola. The oceans couldn't keep trouble at bay. I wished somehow that my friends and I could remove the hurt and pain, secure it in a bottle, and hurl the bottle of pain into the sea. Then the Caribbean Sea and the Atlantic Ocean – total failures as a fortress – could at once carry away the island's trouble.

In the epicenter of despair, I encountered dirty-faced orphans and the hollow stares of newly widowed and bereaved parents. I think they may have all asked, "Dear God, how can this be?"

If the oceans couldn't carry away their worst pain, trepidation, and instability, how would the broken heal? How could the distraught people of Haiti find emotional rest and peace? Where would they find hope and help?

Could such desperately sought healing take place when a

man climbed to the top of the rubble, risked his own life, and shouted words of hope to the men, women, and children trapped below? Maybe it happened when a complete stranger looked at the posted picture of a missing child and allowed tears to flow with the distraught family. Perhaps it occurred when a praying believer pleaded, "Lord, have mercy."

* * * *

Every church I've had a part in is special to me, but Gateway Baptist Church in Tuscola, Texas, is unique among that list. My family, along with four other families, founded Gateway Baptist when we were led by God to start a church in south Taylor County. The Lord used us to point many people to Christ. Seeing His hand move in this way energized us, and He blessed our efforts with a remarkable response and rapid church growth.

One Sunday in 1992, my family gathered in Gateway's sanctuary for worship, Bible study, and prayer. Our pastor stood behind the pulpit making his typical announcements about ongoing ministry and special events. One of those announcements caught my attention. A native Haitian by the name of Jacques Alexandre, a graduate of Arlington Baptist College, was scheduled to visit and share his testimony regarding his ministry to reach the people of Haiti with the message of Christ.

I enjoy meeting people from around the world who are eager to serve the Lord in their home country. While ministry in America is definitely far from boring and the needs are endless, I admire the bravery and courage that ministry demands in places like India, Ukraine, and Haiti. As our pastor finished the announcements, I made a mental note of the date. We rarely missed a Sunday at Gateway, but I wanted to make sure I'd be there to hear Jacques' story.

The Sunday came for Brother Alexandre to speak. Everything was familiar that Sunday except for the man from Port-au-Prince, Haiti, standing behind the pulpit. Jacques had a compelling accent, a contagious energy, and a call for us to imagine life in the Haitian country where people are hungry, poor, illiterate, and in need of the gospel – a gospel that teaches men and women how to be made right with God by faith in Christ Jesus. His message and personality intrigued me, and I looked forward to the opportunity to talk with him.

The Lord opened the door for Nancy and I to develop a relationship with Jacques that very first Sunday with Gateway Baptist. The pastor and Jacques had made arrangements for him to stay in a local hotel. When I heard about it, I offered for Jacques and his wife Marie to stay in our home instead. Having missionaries in our home is a ministry Nancy and I always enjoyed. Jacques accepted our invitation and stayed with us. It was the perfect opportunity for him to share his passion as we fellowshipped in the comfort of our home. God used this time together to place within me a heart for my new friend's ministry in Haiti.

The visit to our home in 1992 was the first of many. A few years later, we received Jacques into our home again, only this time we planned my first trip to his country. The vision for his ministry included building a school and a church. After much prayer and receiving my family's support, I volunteered to assist Jacques with this project.

From that point on, our strong connection grew into a meaningful friendship. The depth of my and Nancy's respect for Jacques and Marie increased quickly. As needs surfaced, Nancy and I found ways to contribute to Jacques' ministry. He knew the Word and demonstrated unwavering commitment to the Lord's call on his life. Not only did I develop a deep love and appreciation for Jacques and Marie, but also a fondness for the Haitian believers.

One of Jacques and Marie's stays fell on our daughter's birthday. Nancy and I try to make birthdays special for our daughters, and having Jacques and Marie at the party made the evening all the more memorable. We made plans to eat at the Beehive, a true Texas steakhouse in downtown Abilene. After sitting down at the table, ordering our steaks, and enjoying the meal, the waiter brought out a piece of cake decorated with a single candle. Jacques and Marie serenaded our daughter by singing Happy Birthday in French:

> *Joyeux anniversaire.*
> *Joyeux anniversaire.*
> *Joyeux anniversaire, Emily.*
> *Joyeux anniversaire.*

Sharing in special meals, church services, and conversations cultivated our friendship and my trust in Jacques. As I have needed prayer, I've called on him, and when he has needed me for prayer, encouragement, and assistance with special projects, I have tried to be available. Eighteen years ago when we first met in that country church, I had no idea of the incredible opportunity God would grant us to bear witness to God's love together.

* * * *

On Tuesday evening, January 12, 2010, I called Jacques and failed to reach him. At 4:53 p.m. a catastrophic 7.0 earthquake had torn Port-au-Prince to shreds. I couldn't feel at peace until I knew Marie and Jacques were safe. Early reports projected incredible loss of life. Later reports confirmed those early projections. The earthquake and aftershocks claimed over three hundred thousand lives.

Early images presented the Haitian capital in distress. In my heart, I was certain the Alexandre home and church would be in the same situation. I prayed God would save their lives and sought comfort in the promise of God's Word. I found assurance in Scripture found in Deuteronomy, *he will not fail thee nor forsake thee.* If the seismic activity destroyed my friend's life and home, Jacques, Marie, and the believers at his church had a mansion waiting in heaven, for those in Christ have the promise of eternity with our Heavenly Father.

I tried to call again after a few hours but still couldn't reach him. I continued to pray for his safety, Marie's safety, and the children's safety. I also prayed, "Lord, allow us to learn the nature of our friends' well-being soon."

The next day I still couldn't get through to Jacques. Because of the disaster, phone lines and electrical lines remained off-line, and communication was nonexistent. Finally, an unbelievable breakthrough in communication occurred.

News crews had made it to Port-au-Prince the night of the earthquake and reported on the damage, loss of life, and great difficulties facing its residents the next day. NBC journalists toured neighborhoods and found, of the millions of people affected, Jacques Alexandre to interview. God found a way to answer my prayer. I received a call informing me of the interview and, quickly, I had Nancy search for the video on the Internet.

There on Nancy's laptop, clear as day, was Jacques Alexandre – white from the dust covering his face and clothing. Incredible relief flooded me. Tears filled our eyes at the sight of Jacques, but I wondered about his family, his church, and the children that received their education at a school operated by Jacques' ministry.

An urgent need to pray washed over me, although not

just to pray but also to go to Port-au-Prince. In spite of my health – I was battling cancer at the time – I couldn't sit in the comfort of my home and enjoy life in the United States while my Haitian friends and their church family suffered. I had to fly to Haiti. People needed food, water, medical supplies, and spiritual encouragement.

In Haiti, Jacques faced a potentially disastrous situation. Marie needed medical attention urgently. Falling concrete had struck her leg and a piece of rebar had cut her. She was extremely fortunate to escape with only a cut, but her condition as a diabetic intensified the need for medical assistance. Jacques felt torn between the condition of his church family and the needs of his wife, but knew what he had to do. Less than a day after the quake, he decided to leave Port-au-Prince for Marie's health and thought it might also be the best way to find help for his church family. He determined to head towards Santo Domingo in the neighboring nation of the Dominican Republic.

Jacques knew the journey would present an untold number of challenges, but he had no choice. The first challenge awaited him in the driveway. A collapsed concrete wall had fallen on part of their car. Until they fixed this, they wouldn't be traveling anywhere. Men from the church chipped in and graciously removed the crumbled concrete and beat out dents in the car frame so the tires could turn freely.

It turned out that Jacques and Marie left Port-au-Prince and headed towards the Dominican Republic to seek medical attention for Marie's wound on the same day he was interviewed by NBC. The farther the two of them traveled from the earthquake's epicenter, the less damage there was. Roads and speed of travel improved significantly. After a hard journey, they arrived in Santo Domingo to look after Marie's leg. Once Jacques secured treatment for the wound, he made his first phone call to the United States.

On January 14, Nancy left a little after 8:00 a.m. to see after our daughter Emily as she neared the delivery of her first child (our third grandchild). While the excitement of the day filled most of our thoughts, I hoped to hear from Jacques soon. As I got ready to make the across-town drive to Hendrick Hospital, an unfamiliar number displayed on my phone's screen. I often don't answer unfamiliar numbers, but this time I felt I should. It was Jacques! I rejoiced to hear his voice and let him start the conversation.

In the course of our call, he informed me that they had decided to leave Port-au-Prince after taking a couple of days to check on the church's members and make the car drivable. What he had to say next was difficult to absorb. "Twenty-seven church members died in the earthquake." His voice grew thick with emotion as he added: "mostly women and children." He went on to share how the earthquake had destroyed the ministry's school buildings. People had little to eat, little clean water to drink, and they were terrified to sleep in buildings because of the aftershocks.

"Dale," Jacques said. "I promised the church that when I came back I would have food and other relief items for them. Can you help me fulfill that promise?"

I confidently assured him of our support and prayers. "Jacques, I will do everything I can. We are here for you."

The two of us thanked the Lord that his family had survived, for we knew his family could have had the same tragic ending as so many others in Haiti. I told Jacques we would help, but I had no idea how.

* * * *

I turned to God's Word for guidance. The Gospel of Matthew contains the account of when Jesus took Peter, James, and John to walk up a mountain. While on the mountain, Jesus allowed the three disciples to see His glory. Based on that passage, the mountain is known as the "Mount of Transfiguration." From the disciples' perspective, at first, Jesus' face looked as it did every day. But in the next instant, His face *did shine as the sun.* A voice from a bright cloud said, *This is My beloved Son, in whom I am well pleased* – the same confirmation announced following Jesus' baptism in the Jordan River. The disciples were terrified when they heard the voice of God and fell face down. Then Jesus touched them and told them to get up and not to be afraid.

Following this powerful moment, as the disciples descended from the mountain and returned to the crowd, a father brought his seizure-ridden son to Jesus for healing. When the Lord healed the boy, the disciples responded in disbelief, for while Jesus was on the mountain, some of Jesus' other disciples had tried to heal the boy without success. It left them asking why couldn't they provide this type of healing.

Jesus responded,

> *If ye have faith as a grain of mustard seed, ye shall say unto this mountain, Remove hence to yonder place; and it shall remove; and nothing shall be impossible unto you* (Matthew 17:20).

This is exactly what I needed in my efforts to assist Jacques and his friends. I needed faith the size of a mustard seed to move the mountain of hurt and despair found in Haiti. I needed this mustard seed-size faith to find a form of transportation, a batch of supplies, and connections in Santo Domingo to get the supplies to Jacques. And this was just a start, because these were only surface issues on top of a mountain of other concerns.

My mustard-seed faith led me to pray, "How can I send aid?" I wanted wisdom and direction. I also asked the Lord to open doors of conversation and prayed for God to open the hearts of those with whom I shared Jacques' request. I decided to move forward in approaching the mountain with the hope of seeing the glory of Jesus shine like the sun.

One week after the earthquake, I drove down North First Street in Abilene and spotted the Global Samaritan Resources building. This is a ministry that provides supplies for every type of need imaginable, with a worldwide reach. Recently, I had met the organization's CEO, Ed Enzor, through Mark Coley, the head football coach at Abilene Christian High School. I served for a few years on Coach Coley's staff as a defensive coordinator, and spent a total of five years coaching the junior varsity and varsity teams. With what God had placed on my heart, I am forever grateful for Coach Coley's introduction.

Seeing the Global Samaritan Resources building, I abruptly switched lanes. My earlier vision of the mustard seed and mountain compelled me to go see Mr. Enzor. I pulled into the parking lot and walked inside. Each step was a step of faith. I had no idea what I would say or do. What I did know was that I felt a strong urging to stop by his office. That I couldn't ignore.

I asked the receptionist at the front desk for "Mr. Ed." For the life of me, I couldn't remember his last name. (Doctors tell me the treatment for my illness can cause memory loss. It's a convenient scapegoat.) Fortunately, the receptionist, who knew I wasn't looking for a talking palomino from the 1960s television show, directed me down a corridor to Ed Enzor's office.

I followed the hall to his office, but when I arrived at his door, I heard him talking on the phone. Not wanting to interrupt, I listened to the conversation standing outside the door. From Ed's side of the conversation, I discerned he and the other person on the line (I later learned was a vice president with ExxonMobil) were discussing how to take lifesaving supplies to Haiti via the Dominican Republic. All supplies would route through the Dominican Republic due to the destroyed runways of Toussaint Louverture International Airport near Port-au-Prince. God was confirming that my mustard seed of faith was beginning to move a mountain.

When I peeked in the door, Ed waved me into his office. His phone conversation continued – it was apparent they needed someone on the ground in Santo Domingo. God uses both bad and good for his purposes, but this had me shaking my head. Jacques just so happened to be in Santo Domingo getting medical treatment for his wife's injuries, and he had previously served with Ron Valero, a missionary in the Dominican Republic. Now Jacques and Marie were resting at the Valero home. They would wait in Santo Domingo for God to provide a way to get supplies back to their church members in Port-au-Prince.

I raised my hand. Ed told the person on the other end of the line to "Hold on for a second." Then he asked me, "Dale, do you know someone in Santo Domingo?" Without hesitation, I said, "Yes." He returned to the conversation: "The Lord just provided someone on the ground."

The phone conversation lasted a few minutes longer with discussion about how to get through customs, travel on the ground, and a host of other issues to consider. Then Ed looked at me and said, "Dale, ExxonMobil will provide a jet and pilots to fly supplies to Santo Domingo. We need someone to get them from the plane to Port-au-Prince. Can you go?" There was no time to pray, call Nancy, or talk to my numerous doctors. I said, "Yes, I can go."

Once I agreed, I received a whirlwind of instructions. The ExxonMobil jet would be in Abilene the following day for loading supplies. I had twenty-four hours to secure transportation and trucks in the Dominican Republic as well as personal funds for the trip. I completely trusted God to move the mountain as I held onto my mustard seed-size faith.

Walking in on that conversation brought on an adrenaline rush and a sense of expectation. I had no doubt God was orchestrating a plan in which I would play a part. Even so, I dreaded calling Nancy to tell her that her husband – with a medical history a mile long and a compromised immune system – would soon be en route to a poor country ravaged by a terrible earthquake with an untold number of injuries, complicated by rampant infections.

I made the call to Nancy and went through a list of things God had done that morning to get relief to people in Haiti. I took a deep breath and continued with details about all the people God was using, and finished by telling her I would be the one taking the supplies to Haiti.

Nancy said nothing. The silence lasted for a few seconds but felt much longer. She said, "I understand why you need to do this." We said good-bye, expressed our love, and hung up. In my heart, I thanked God, for I knew her reaction was another work of God.

Two minutes later, Nancy called back with a list of appropriate questions I had yet to consider. Where are you going to stay? How will we communicate? How will you get back home? The last question was of tremendous importance in the list of questions because the corporate jet with its three pilots would leave as soon as the supplies were unloaded in the Dominican Republic.

With our new list of challenges identified, Nancy, who has been a true helpmate throughout our marriage, went to work arranging a flight home. I went to work establishing contact with Jacques. I couldn't wait to let him know about the miracle coming by way of an Exxon Mobil jet! Two days before we were to leave for Santo Domingo, I reached Jacques with the news and he shouted with joy.

Upon coordinating further with Jacques, I turned my energy

to gathering, inspecting, and loading supplies. When I arrived at the airport the next morning, I couldn't believe the quality and amount of supplies. The provisions included baby formula, food, water, medicine, a generator, and five water purification systems. The value of all the supplies totaled a quarter-million dollars. A crew removed all but two of the seats from the plane to make space for the cargo. The pilots sat in the cockpit, and a third Exxon Mobile employee sat in a fold-down chair.

While inspecting the supplies, a man I didn't know approached the jet. He introduced himself as Ben Gray and told me of his desire to travel on the jet to Haiti. A college professor at Abilene Christian University and a volunteer at Global Samaritan, Ben had the calling and training to provide significant help. I let him know that the decision was not mine, because I didn't own the plane. After a couple of minutes of talking with those coordinating the effort, the coordinators made the decision – Ben *would* go with me to Haiti. It felt good to have a companion for the trip. Ben's arrival reminded me of Jesus sending out the disciples in pairs. We would be better off going together. After completing the loading process, the plane left for Dallas to complete final clearances for the hastily coordinated flight hauling lifesaving provisions to Santo Domingo.

The next morning, January 22, Ben and I said good-bye to our wives at the Abilene airport and flew on American Airlines to Dallas. Once in Dallas, an ExxonMobil representative took us to the jet filled with supplies ready to save countless lives by providing food, medicine, and the possibility of clean water. Without much fanfare, we boarded the loaded plane in Dallas and took a direct flight to Santo Domingo in the Dominican Republic. Ben, three pilots, and I flew over the Gulf of Mexico at thirty-two thousand feet. The whole experience felt like a dream. I asked Ben to pinch my arm to make sure the whole thing was real. I can only describe it as a feeling one has when the mustard seed feels the mountain moving.

Thirty minutes into the flight, one of the pilots brought us a breakfast tray with various fruits, and we devoured it. A couple hours later, another pilot placed enough food on our trays to feed the masses. The selection included breads, meats, cheese, and nuts. Overall, we received royal CEO-like treatment from the pilots. Ben and I looked at the quantity of food and decided to save some of it for our travel in Haiti since we didn't know when we'd eat like this again.

The landing in Santo Domingo confirmed to me even more that God's hand was upon our efforts every step of the way. As soon as the plane completed its taxiing, officials and security met us. The officials boarded the plane asking for our paperwork. None of the officials spoke fluent English, and no one on our team spoke great Spanish. Regardless, they seemed to understand we were there to help the earthquake victims.

We really were uncertain how the officials would receive us, thinking that they might confiscate the supplies, demand a bribe, or ask us to return home. We were prepared to pay thousands for the bribe. It would be worth it to get the supplies into the hands of the untold thousands of hungry and thirsty victims. A security official who had gone into the airport office walked back onto the plane with a smile on his face. He said, "I need ten dollars." We gladly handed over the ten dollars.

About an hour after landing, Ben and I disembarked from the plane. I spotted Jacques and Ron Valero standing on the other side of the airport fence. I figured we'd have to endure a customs search before the officers would open the gate so we could leave the airport. Ben and I approached the gates with the supplies loaded on trailers, while the same security official from the airport walked with us. The man ordered the gate to be opened with *no* inspection required. He flashed the same smile as he had earlier when he asked for ten dollars on the plane. As we approached Brother Valero, Jacques shouted, "John Wayne has shown up with the Cavalry! Praise the Lord!"

With so much of the journey ahead of us, we quickly loaded the supplies onto a large U-Haul-like truck. Ron and his wife, Kathy, led us to a local warehouse to purchase eight pallets of food and water. From there, we went back to Ron's house and prepared to leave early the next morning.

Once at Brother Ron's home, Jacques briefed us on what might happen at the border. He said officials could inspect the truck, take what they wanted, or demand large fees to transport the supplies across the border. The next morning, January 23, Ben, Jacques, Ron, and I left the safety of Santo Domingo at 4:00 a.m. to head west on Route 2 towards Port-au-Prince in a moving truck and Ron's jeep.

The closer we came to the border, the more our anxiety rose. I prayed that we would make it through the crossing without interference or problems, just as we'd experienced when passing through customs the previous day. When we reached the Jimani border crossing, we found chaos. Trucks and people moved about like a disturbed nest of frantically swarming fire ants. The line for semi-trucks crossing the border for relief aid backed up for over a mile. We avoided this line and went to the lane for non-commercial traffic. After a short stop at the border, it was as if God's angels opened up the gate, and the armed guards waved us through without asking for an inspection or bribes. Our wild journey into Haiti continued.

By this time it was around 11:00 a.m., and an eight-hour trip still remained. I didn't need mileage signs to tell me where we were. I knew exactly when Port-au-Prince was not far off. The devastation was easily the worst I'd ever seen. We entered a country that had lost, according to estimates, at least 230,000 of its citizens, and at most, 316,000. Another 300,000 were injured. Seven hundred and sixty thousand would suffer from cholera. One hundred and twenty-two Americans died. One thousand orphans would eventually come to the United States as provided through the Help Haiti Act.

When we were about twenty miles from the city's center, the devastation engulfed us. People cried out in pain, they were particularly scared of the dark, and they were searching desperately for food and clean water. Crews worked to remove people buried underneath the concrete jungle. The city had no electricity and no mobile phone coverage.

Our team made it to Jacques' compound Saturday evening. I had visited this piece of Haiti once before over twenty years earlier when Jacques had invited me to assist him in the early stages of building a church and school. The land was vacant at the time. His site for the future ministry was on high ground in Port-au-Prince with two-and three-story concrete houses extending from the property boundaries in every direction as far as I could see. The only building on the ministry's property then was a hut the security guard lived in to prevent squatters from establishing a residence on the land.

Haiti, at that time, was a very unsettling place to visit. Jacques and his neighbors lived in fear of potential break-ins or riots. An eight-foot wall with shards of glass cemented into the surface at the wall's top surrounded his house. Inside the house, a bullhorn sat on the coffee table. I thought it was an odd table decoration and asked why he had it. Jacques informed me the bullhorn was to alert the neighbors of a home invasion. It was the Haitian version of a home security system.

The first evening of my stay I observed the neighbors as they marched in the street carrying guns, machetes, and spears to show they would not be intimated by potential thugs. The difficulties of that first journey to Haiti were child's play compared to what I now surveyed.

As we exited from our vehicle, Jacques' friends, family, and church members were thrilled to see us, but the weariness, pain, and sadness due to the disaster hung like a heavy dew over a meadow. Church members mourned the loss of twenty-seven of their own no longer worshiping among them. I met a Port-au-Prince police officer who carried with him a picture of his young daughter. Through a translator, he explained to me that his daughter died in the earthquake when a wall fell on her. I put my arm around the man's shoulders. He wept while we prayed together.

I recognized faces and reacquainted myself with those I had met on my first trip to Haiti. The stories of tragedy kept coming. Our arrival created a sense of relief and release.

After Jacques had time to greet his church members, we prepared to disperse a portion of the supplies from the truck to Jacques' church family first. A new sense of hope and joy washed across their dust-covered faces at the sight of fresh food and water. We were so exhausted from our trip that we decided to announce that night that the supplies for the neighbors would go out the following day when we'd have morning light and, for ourselves, fresh energy.

On Sunday morning, in order to prevent a stampede of people for the supplies during distribution, some men worked to repair the walls and gates. While they worked, other men and women separated the food into plastic bags with enough food to last one week.

People were desperate for food and nourishment. With our arrival, a new sense of hope and joy shined in their eyes. Since many families built their homes just a few feet from their neighbors or shared a concrete wall with them, many homes had collapsed like a falling domino train. For those whose homes remained intact, they feared returning to retrieve what little food they had in their pantries. Even if a person's home was secure, they most likely only had enough food for a day or two, since most Haitian homemakers visit the market each day for their food.

When it came time to distribute the bags of food, people crowded in front of the gates to receive food. Well over a thousand people from the neighborhood gathered with the hope that they'd be able to feed their families. With little space to gather outside the church walls, the crowd stretched out a half-mile amidst the broken concrete.

From the back of the crowd, an elderly lady close to the church fence struggled to make her way to the front of the horde. I grabbed a bullhorn and handed it to the interpreter. "Tell the crowd to pass this bag of food to the lady in the back."

I'm not sure if the lady was a widow, but the Bible has plenty to say about taking care of the weak and fragile among us. Even though most people in the crowd had not read those Scriptures, the Lord calmed the people and their own integrity overcame the desire to take care of self before others. It surprised me that someone didn't try to take the bag and run off. Slowly and calmly, each person handed the bag to the next person in line, until the bag reached the lady.

After the first day of distribution and worship, night fell and people slept outside on the ground and on cots, enduring the constant nuisance of swarming mosquitos. The darkness was the blackest dark I had ever experienced. We had no way to generate light. Not being able to see was unnerving, and each morning everyone felt relieved to see the sunrise.

On that Sunday afternoon, Jacques led his church members and other folks from the surrounding area in worship on the church grounds. The people crowded into the yard near the demolished church. With no church building to meet in, the people gathered under tarps to find relief from the sun. Jacques had asked me to preach. My message focused on how God can bring good out of tragedies. I encouraged the people to look for that good in the days to come. "God allowed the Israelites to rebuild Jerusalem after the city's destruction at the hands of the Babylonians, and I can see God doing the same thing in Haiti." That day, the Lord added to His church, as eleven people in the overflow crowd trusted Christ for salvation.

Jesus taught in the gospels that if a believer has faith the size of a mustard seed, mountains could move by the command of our voice. The mustard seed of our faith lay at the base of an incredible mountain. A thought occurred to me that the mountain before me was greater than any previous mountain in my life. A mountain of this magnitude grew even larger because the suffering was not that of a few but of an entire nation. Haiti was in shock, and those in Christ, Jacques, Ron, Ben, Ed and Global Samaritan had, as quickly as possible, brought light into a very dark and difficult situation.

I prayed the supplies would allow Jacques' church to be a stronghold and a place of hope for those living near the church. The crowd received food on Sunday morning and an invitation for worship Sunday afternoon. The gathering assembled for Sunday afternoon was larger than the number of people who had received food. People needed physical food to regain their strength, but they also needed a filling of the reserves of hope, faith, and belief in God's sustaining presence. During the service, people cried, sang, listened to the sermon, and grew stronger spiritually. The food had brought renewed strength, while the worship service that January Sunday furthered the recovery of hope in the assurance of God's presence.

On Sunday evening, people milled around the church while others continued the nonstop search-and-rescue efforts. The two past days had brought renewed hope for the people, but they were still thirsty and there was precious little drinking water available. The water we brought quickly ran out. Almost every water well and cistern was destroyed. Haitians gathered water any way they could when a rain shower fell, but this was only a drop in the perpetual bucket of thirst.

The United States military tried to address the need for clean drinking water. I observed this firsthand the day before when a military helicopter hovered above a field while soldiers dropped ropes to the ground. After securing a perimeter, the soldiers lowered a pallet of bottled water. The soldiers returned to the helicopter seconds after the pallet settled. The result was heartbreaking, because without soldiers to ensure orderly distribution, chaos broke out as parched men swarmed the water. Only the strongest and the quickest left with water to return to their thirsty children and injured family members.

Since people had supported Global Samaritan financially, ExxonMobil let us use its jet and by the mercy of God, Ben and I had an answer to the water shortage. We had brought five water purification systems with us, and Ben had received training in both their set-up and operation. Sunday evening was the first time we demonstrated how the systems worked.

A large crowd desperate for clean drinking water gathered around us and the equipment. We set one system at the church and another by the remains of a six-story hospital where patients had been moved to parking lots and onto the lawn.

After setting up all five of the systems, we shifted our focus to our return trip home, arriving safely in Santo Domingo on Monday afternoon, thirteen days after the earthquake.

Ben and I returned to America with images sewn into our memory that didn't allow us to rest. Comforts like running water, refrigerated food, and secure homes seemed almost extravagant as we considered the immense difficulties facing our new friends in Haiti. We raised funds, encouraged participation in a return trip, and collected more supplies. Many were eager to help and a few were even willing to go.

Men from Abilene churches joined me in a return trip to Haiti with new supplies and medicine still in high demand a month later. My experience in Haiti under normal circumstances and then under catastrophic circumstances made me the natural leader for the trip. Flying out of Dallas, I took time to prepare the group for what they would see in Haiti, and how God would use us to bring hope and help into a very dark place.

Upon arriving in Haiti, the team saw firsthand how sickness, hunger, and thirst continued to make Haiti a place of desolation. Even though several weeks had passed since the earthquake, the nighttime cries of hurting people haunted us.

Our team of nine included a pediatrician from Abilene who enlisted two in our group to operate as pharmacists. Mobs of people gathered to receive medical care and medicine. Some had cuts, infections, broken limbs, burns, and suffered from dehydration. The team worked around the clock offering prayers, treatment, and medicine.

We also distributed hundreds of solar-powered flashlights to the people who came through the clinics. With so many Haitians without power, every person receiving a flashlight reacted like a kid on Christmas morning. It was remarkable to see neighborhoods change from pitch-black streets to avenues of light. The lights provided the expected practical benefits but also gave a greater sense of security.

Moving around Haiti was extremely challenging due to precious few drivable roads as we moved from site to site in a rented van. We moved quicker because of the medical services made available by the people on our team. By sticking my head out the window and yelling, "Doctor on board!" the police quickly directed traffic out of our way. It was amazing what a pair of medical scrubs and a stethoscope around my neck could do in clearing a road.

Traveling at night was easier because people stayed off the

roads, but it was also much more dangerous due to gangs and thieves stopping cars. The thieves tried to steal from groups like ours, making their money by selling supplies for one hundred percent profit. On the day before we were to return to the Dominican Republic, we had stayed too long at a site where we administered medical aid and were forced to drive at night. The trip back to the church was going well until we noticed bright flames in the road ahead. The closer we drove to the fire it became evident that we were driving towards an ambush roadblock of burning tires. It was too late to turn around so I yelled to the driver, "Speed up! Speed up! Drive through it!"

Right before we drove through the burning tires, a rock flew through the van's window. It wasn't until we were safely through the tires that I looked back to make sure no one was injured. I was in awe of what I discovered. The van had been completely full except for one seat. The thieves failed to cause harm with the rock because it flew through the window next to the only empty seat. The seat was vacant because John Whitten, the college pastor at Pioneer Drive Baptist Church in Abilene and a member of our team, had decided to move to the backseat since we no longer had it full of supplies. If the rock had hit John or the intended target, which was most likely our driver, the rock's size would have caused significant injury. I added this saving grace to our list of miracles.

We made it safely to Jacques' church and eventually to our homes in Texas.

Our two trips provided both spiritual and physical blessings to people who were hurting and mourning. Many people came to know Christ through our ministry, including the man who drove us from Santo Domingo to Port-au-Prince on our second trip. He wrote me a note that I carry in my Bible to this day as a cherished memory.

The one event above all the rest that significantly altered the recovery process was the day people had clean water to drink. It was on my first trip with Ben. We needed a water source to run through the water purification system – this was less than two weeks after the earthquake and water delivery was out of the question. Someone mentioned taking water from the baptistery, but when Ben went to examine it, it was green with algae. We decided the system should work well enough to clean this water, so we retrieved enough water with buckets to try it and covered the baptistery with tin to keep dust and trash out of the remaining water for future use. Ben pumped the baptistery water once used to celebrate new life in Christ into the system.

As clean, filtered water flowed, the people looked around to see who would test it to see if the water was fit to drink. No one came forward. Up until this point, I had only consumed bottled water, but Ben decided we needed to lead. I agreed with him. We had brought the systems. We needed to drink the water. I took a drink with Ben. The water tasted of chlorine but otherwise it appeared to be fine.

Even after our initiative in drinking the water, we were the only ones who seemed interested. Finally, a Haitian lady came forward ready to take a try. Her decision brought about a willingness to do the same among her friends and relatives. One at a time, people walked towards the faucet to fill gallon Ziploc bags with water. Smiles, all of a sudden, became contagious. Those in desperate need of drinkable water now had access to a system that could pump out five hundred gallons a day of clean water. The sip of water not only brought hope to the Haitian people but would also change my life forever.

2

THE WALLS FALL

On September 10, 2001, I drove away from our home in Tuscola headed to a new home site to complete the final grade of dirt work. As I turned onto the county road, my thoughts circled back to my mother, Delores. I'd struggled all morning to shake the nervous tension building. Mama had recently discovered a knot in her neck, and it turned out to be a tumor. She was having surgery that day at Baylor Hospital in Garland, Texas, to diagnose the tumor.

I arrived at the work site, jumped on a backhoe, and started moving dirt in a futile attempt to channel my thoughts in a different direction. Blissfully losing myself in my work, I spent the first half of the day on the backhoe. After lunch, I climbed back aboard the backhoe and worked until I received the call I had waited for all day from my sister, Lorraine. Her report wasn't what we had hoped and prayed for. "Mama has cancer," she said. It was difficult news, and the difficulty only intensified when she said, "It's non-Hodgkin's lymphoma. The tumor can't be removed surgically due to its location and size."

The most challenging bit of news came at the end of our conversation. "The doctor says Mama has three months to live, according to his best guess."

The news hit me hard. "Tell Mama that I love her, and we'll see her tomorrow."

With hardly a thought as to what God might do for Mama, uncertainty and hopelessness took the driver's seat of my spirit for a few minutes. I sat on the backhoe in disbelief. The news wasn't about a woman I worked with at a previous job or about some lady from our church family. This was my God-fearing mother we were talking about – the kindest, most gentle lady I'd ever known – and she had terminal cancer. I sat in shock.

After a moment of gloom, I regrouped and regained my faith footing. I took my concerns to my Savior who is the Great Physician. I asked Him to intervene and prayed, "Lord give me a word of hope for my family."

I decided to complete the job for that day since I wasn't sure when I might return from Garland. Over the next few hours on that September afternoon, I felt the Lord saying, "More time, more time." God granted me the assurance that these words would encourage Nancy and my children as I prepared to tell them that our very dear mother and grandmother had terminal cancer.

I drove home in a numb state. Memories of times with my mother flashed through my mind. Whether the Lord would give us three months or longer, I knew the Lord had blessed me abundantly with the mother He gave me.

* * * *

My mom's life was remarkable for many reasons. She had to grow up fast, had held her own against my strong-willed father, and had cultivated her faith later than most. From where my mother lay in her hospital room, she wasn't all that far from her childhood home. Mama grew up outside of Garland but not quite in Rowlett, Texas. In her teenage years, she and her friends frequented the Payne's Drug Store in Garland to enjoy refreshments from the ice cream parlor and soda fountain. On one afternoon, when she was only fourteen, a mischievous older boy she didn't know decided to show his interest in my mother by dropping a June bug down the neck of her dress. She made sure he knew she didn't appreciate it.

Despite the initial failed attempt at romance, my mother forgave Dale Morrison for his antics, and they started to date. Eventually, they married, in spite of opposition voiced from those who knew them.

My father was a Texas boy who grew up in Malakoff, Texas until the age of nine. His dad delivered mail for the U.S. Postal Service for twenty-one years in the Malakoff area before moving the family to Garland. Every morning my grandfather left my grandmother to be with their rambunctious son who wanted nothing more than to ride with his father on the mail route. Seeing that my dad wouldn't give in to my grandfather telling him he could not do this, my grandfather approached his supervisor with his then-seven-year-old boy in tow.

"Tell him what you want to do, Dale," my grandfather encouraged.

My dad boldly requested, "Sir, can I please ride with Daddy when he delivers the mail?"

The supervisor flatly declined. "Son, we have laws forbidding your request. If you want to ride with your father, you'll have to ask permission from the President of the United States!"

That's exactly what Dad did. He wrote a letter to democrat President Franklin Roosevelt requesting permission. President Roosevelt, or a White House staffer, took time out, even with World War II going on, to respond to someone who couldn't even vote yet. The letter encouraged Dad to do his best in school and to assist in the war effort by collecting scrap metal and tires. In regards to riding in a U.S. Postal Service truck, to my father's dismay, our wartime president stood behind the law and declined my father's request. I think this is why Dad voted mostly Republican.

My father attended public schools in Garland until the ninth grade. During one lunch recess, he and a few friends engaged in a harmless wrestling match. A teacher came around the corner and believed she had a fight to break up. She alerted the school principal and took the group of rabble-rousers to the office. My dad pled innocent as he tried to explain that the teacher misunderstood what was actually taking place.

The principal stood behind the teacher and decided to administer swats. Dad stubbornly resisted. "I didn't do anything wrong," he said. "I will not let you give me a swat." My dad's friends, however, complied. Due to my dad's resistance, the principal kicked him out of the public education system. Dad took a few days to mull over his options and decided to enlist in the United States Navy.

Dad was seventeen and Mama was fourteen when they decided to get married after two months of dating. In order to get the marriage license, both the bride and groom were to receive a physical. They both went to see the local doctor. My dad's physical proceeded routinely, but the doctor couldn't look past my mother's age. He tried to talk my mother out of moving forward with my father's proposal. "If you get married at your age, the marriage won't last two months." My parents didn't heed the warning and proceeded with the wedding, blinded, I suppose, by love and youth.

On February 23, 1952, with the written consent of each parent, Dale and Delores exchanged vows in Garland. Dad had convinced Mama to honeymoon at my great-grandparents' house south of Malakoff. According to my mother, Dad described the house as a sort of mansion – he promised it would be very enjoyable.

To her disappointment, Mama spent her first three wedded nights in a dilapidated farmhouse with a leaky roof. To make the situation more unsettling, one of Dad's cousins and her husband came to visit and made themselves welcome for a few hours. Mama waited a few years to tell Dad how miserably he failed in accurately describing their honeymoon destination.

After the honeymoon, my parents adjusted to life as newlyweds. Dad had commitments to the Navy and received San Diego as his post. Dad left Mom behind and arranged for her to travel to San Diego by bus. Once she arrived, the newlyweds settled into their West Coast home. Dad left for months at a time. Eventually, the Navy deployed dad's ship to fight in the Korean War, and Mom returned to Garland.

After fulfilling his commitment to the navy, my parents focused on establishing roots and starting a family. On July 13, 1958, my mom went into labor, and hours later, I came into the world. My parents said I was a typical baby – not too tranquil nor too colicky. They went on to have two more children, Dwayne and Lorraine.

The older I grew the more I exhibited the Morrison attribute of stubbornness. My mother and father learned this early on. For example, my parents consistently warned me to never step off the curb onto the street. One day, as my Dad tells it, I was playing outside by myself. I looked around the yard to see if anyone was watching and walked to the curb. For several minutes, I walked up and down the curb contemplating my next move. I took a second look scanning for potential surveillance. Once I believed the coast to be clear, off the curb I went. My dad watched the entire incident from the living room window. He raced outside, scolded me, and gave me my first of many spankings.

I can say without question and without much argument from my dad that Mama provided unconditional, gentle love for

Dwayne, Lorraine, and me. She made every birthday special for me by cooking my favorite egg-custard pie. Mama also worked hard to make the holidays special. But she didn't just show that love on special occasions. Her love permeated everyday life. For instance, she always had a snack waiting for Dwayne and me when we returned home from school. When my dad and I argued, Mama tried to soothe the hurt feelings. She kept the family together through tough times. On the day I left home for good, she made sure I knew how much she loved me as her son. I never took that love for granted.

* * * *

On that September day in 2001, after learning about Mama's cancer when conversing with Lorraine, I pulled into our driveway, overcome with sentiment from reminiscing. I walked through the office door and hugged Nancy. I held on to her for a little longer than usual. All three of our daughters were there. Nancy had called Courtney and Emily after their college classes and told them to come home for the evening. By the looks on their faces, they both suspected something was wrong.

Nancy picked up the phone to call my parents in Garland. My mother answered. Always the calm, assuring presence, she sounded fine. However, my father, always the bull in a china shop, was losing it. He had Mama halfway in the grave already.

I prayed with Mama over the phone and after saying good-bye, I gathered my three daughters and Nancy in our bedroom and shared the doctor's report with them.

The girls loved their Grandma very much and tried to respond the best they could to the news. They prayed and cried together, and we all decided to fast and pray for the rest of the evening, asking God to intervene in a miraculous way. We spent several hours together that evening resting in the comfort of each other's presence.

The next day, after praying more than I slept, I believed the Lord had something different in mind from what the doctor had told my mother, father, and sister. I was grateful for how God encouraged me with His Word given to me by His Holy Spirit.

The Holy Spirit is God's Presence dwelling inside the follower of Christ. According to Ephesians 1:13, the Spirit's indwelling occurs after we hear the gospel proclaimed and then upon believing its claims turn to Jesus for our salvation. The Bible also claims that the saved man or woman receives life by the Holy Spirit. This same life resurrected Jesus from the tomb near Jerusalem.

God as Holy Spirit is also the identifier of our soul's belonging to the Father. Allow me to offer an illustration of how this works. When I became the first child of Dale and Delores Morrison in July of 1958, I received a birth certificate. The birth certificate, along with a Social Security number, was how the United States government guaranteed my identity. The Holy Spirit or divine Counselor acts on my behalf in a similar fashion. The Holy Spirit who descended upon early followers of Christ in Acts 2 is the way God the Father identifies my loyalty to Him. I am a child of God because the Holy Spirit dwells within me. Not only that, the Holy Spirit is a source of strength in times of weakness.

Nancy and I climbed into the car ready to go to Garland, but before starting our car, I felt the Holy Spirit working in my mind. He didn't allow me to believe the doctor's initial conclusions. I shared what God laid on my heart as Nancy and I made our way to Garland, and felt the visit would also lift my spirits.

As we neared Eastland, Texas, traveling east on Interstate 20, a DJ for KGNZ radio interrupted programming to request listeners to pray because an airplane had struck one of the World

Trade Center towers in lower Manhattan. The DJ assured listeners that more information would follow and encouraged people to pray for those in the building and for emergency personnel hurrying to the scene. Nancy looked at me with disbelief and said, "How could that happen?"

Not long after the first breaking-news announcement, the DJ alerted us that a second plane had crashed into the south tower of the World Trade Center. He further reported that government officials suspected a terrorist attack. Nancy and I neared the Metroplex area and decided to take I-20 south of downtown Dallas in case the attacks spread to other urban centers. Within a twenty-four-hour period, my family and the country my dad served in the United States Navy were under attack. My family's attacker was cancer, while al-Qaeda and radical Islam had launched a surprise attack upon American citizens in New York and Washington, D.C.

After finally making it to Baylor Hospital following a bewildering and stressful drive, we took the elevator to Mama's room. I prepared myself to stay strong as we walked into the room. Mama lay on the bed with Lorraine, Dwayne, and Dad standing nearby. She smiled a beautiful smile and greeted us warmly. I hugged my siblings and Dad and took my place by Mama's side.

A news reporter on the television broke in on our reunion and relayed information about the tragedy developing miles away from the uncertain situation in my mom's hospital room. Video clips of planes flying into the World Trade Center towers and collapsing buildings played repeatedly. People fled the towers and surrounding buildings, running down the dust-covered streets of lower Manhattan.

In Mama's hospital room, we witnessed the greatest city in the world receive a potential knockout blow. We stared in disbelief as those trapped in the upper floors of the towers determined their best option was to jump. Mama broke the silence with inherent wisdom. She pointed towards the television and said, "Dale Richard, the doctor told me that I have three months to live, but those people don't have tomorrow." Richard is my middle name and my family always uses Richard to distinguish me from my father.

I replied, "Mama, that's what I love about you. You always think of others before yourself." We turned from the attack in New York to cancer's attack on my mother's body.

My father shared with me what I already knew from my sister. The cancer in Mama's body was advanced, and her situation was essentially hopeless. After roughly ten minutes of conversation, I said, "Dad, maybe God has a different plan."

After an encouraging time with the Lord the day before, God had given me a message of hope that he would give all of us more time to enjoy mom alive. I tried to offer an encouraging word, convinced that God wanted to foster hope in the midst of uncertainty.

As I always trust God's timing to be perfect, Dr. Jairo Olivares, Mama's oncologist, walked in at the end of the conversation. He had taken a second look at the most recent lab work and felt better about the prognosis moving forward. Chemotherapy would start as soon as possible, and they would see how Mama progressed.

Dr. Olivares' news had given me a dose of hope in addition to what the Lord impressed upon me, and we all took the opportunity to thank the Lord for his allowance of treatment and time. The news also gave everyone the assurance that our family could make many more memories. We circled around my mother's bed and prayed, "To God be the glory for great things he hath done."

After the prayer, all of us agreed that time together as family was essential from this point forward. The obligations and events that once kept us too busy to gather as a family no longer took priority over time with my Mom. I wanted to have as much time with her as possible and desired the same for my daughters.

* * * *

In our conversation about how to spend the remaining weeks and months, the urge to return to a special place for our family summoned all of us to a place we called "the farm." The farm wasn't far from the sight of my parents' honeymoon "mansion." It was situated three miles south of Malakoff, Texas. After driving across the railroad tracks in Malakoff, you quickly find yourself past the city limits, among trees taller than four-story buildings, rolling terrain with grass-covered pastures, and an abundance of water compared to the often dry, mesquite tree-filled Taylor County countryside in West Texas. It provided simple pleasures like star gazing, fishing for bass and catfish, and riding four-wheelers. Green pastures and orchards served as a refuge. The farm bound together years of delightful memories we all held dear.

The farm was a part of a larger section of East Texas terrain with family ties that had existed for over a century. My great-great-grandfather, Hawk Foster, owned the land and divided it among his sons and daughters. My great-grandparents, Big Daddy and Big Mama, then left the land to my grandmother, Noirene Morrison. My father currently owned the land that had stayed with the family for five generations.

Dad later bought a green one-room cabin for six hundred dollars and had it delivered to the farm. He had it set a mile or so down the county road from the house my parents honeymooned in. It served as a guesthouse. My parents, siblings, and I spent many weekends enjoying the farm. When I was a kid, the trips from Garland to Malakoff began by loading up in the back of the family pickup and then making the two-hour trip in the pickup's bed.

Being at the farm meant fun, but it also meant work. Almost anything grew in the farm's fertile ground. Gardens of watermelons, corn, peas, and potatoes, orchards of pears and peaches, and vines loaded with grapes were commonplace. Dwayne, Dad, and I worked cows, cleared pasture, and repaired fences. When the work ended, Dwayne and I moved ungoverned through the pasture and woods exploring the land on horseback, swinging from tree branches, swimming in ponds, and hunting wild game. The Malakoff farm was a young boy's paradise.

After a full day of work and exploring, Dwayne and I returned to the cabin to clean up for supper and bed. At the farm, we bathed in a tub on the front porch filled with water warmed in the house by a wood-burning stove. As young boys, we feared that a passing motorist might see more than we desired. If we heard even the faintest hum of a car's engine, we darted inside.

My dad happened to be soaking in the bath one evening when a car was about to pass by our cabin. Dad quickly emerged from the tub and darted to the door only to find it locked. Without a towel or garment to cover himself, he hunkered down close to the porch floor. He must have heard the roaring laughter coming from inside the cabin. For all these reasons and more, I lived for weekend trips to the farm.

As I approached my high school years, the farm and the boyhood utopia pulled at me less. I started a mowing business, became active in church activities, and found success in high school sports. I made the occasional trip to the farm to visit family who lived in the Malakoff area and to check on the place as time permitted. As the frequency of visits dwindled, the memories of my childhood grew in sentimental value.

After marrying Nancy and starting our family, I tried to introduce my wife and the girls to life at the farm. On one visit,

Emily, Courtney, and I had gone out to the farm with their Granddaddy and planned to stay the night in the green cabin. I envisioned a bonding time with the girls. A steady rain set in which made for great football watching on an old black and white television with rabbit ears wrapped in tinfoil. During the game, Courtney let me know that she needed to go to the bathroom. The only problem is the cabin had no inside toilet.

This didn't rattle me. Outdoor urination is something young boys embrace enthusiastically, but my girls had a fondness for warm seats and indoor plumbing. We had no choice but to sprint in a downpour to the dreaded outhouse. My rain-soaked, eldest daughter stared at me wide-eyed, scared for her life as we swatted away spider webs and daddy long legs. Did I mention my girls detest bugs? Both Courtney and I survived the outhouse and made it back in to watch the rest of the game.

The farm never lost its importance to my family, but finding the time to get there wasn't always feasible. The drive from Abilene, where I settled after high school, to Malakoff was long. The living arrangements once we arrived were primitive. Outhouses, cold showers, and scheduled bathroom trips into town for those who dared not enter an outhouse were common. No one altogether forgot the farm, but life changed and other things took priority. Trying to make a living, church ministry involvement, and weekend activities for our three daughters made it difficult to make regular visits.

The farm had always provided a place for the family to reconnect. However, with everyone chasing agendas, the opportunities to connect dwindled. We were doing good if everyone got together for Thanksgiving and Christmas. Mama's diagnosis changed all that. When the family found out my mother had non-Hodgkin's lymphoma, the need to reconnect reached new levels of urgency.

My parents never stopped going to the farm to check on

things and keep the place up, but now they had a much bigger group joining them on their occasional visits. Even if it meant sleeping in tents or enclosed trailers, everyone went and enjoyed themselves around the campfire, devouring roasted marshmallows, and listening to the coyotes howl under star-filled skies. The farm has that kind of romantic appeal. It's been in the family since the 1800s and it beats the hurry-up-and-wait of city life.

For newcomers to the family, it provides a nice getaway. For my family of origin, the farm is a place that allows an escape, not just *from* the hectic life, but also *into* the memories of an easier time when no one had cancer, burdens, or fear.

Our sentimentalities for the farm in no way curbed the family's stubborn streak from entering the property. I remember some competitive touch football games and domino marathons, but time at the farm also gave us time to unwind in ways our daily schedules did not normally allow. For instance, if you wanted to swing in a hammock, you swung away. If you had a hankering to climb into the treehouse, you climbed. If you enjoyed staring into a fire for an hour, no one tracked your time.

As Mama's cancer worsened, she made fewer trips to the farm, but my siblings and I still felt it important to spend time together as a family at the Malakoff farm. We made plans to build a two-story cabin near the biggest pond on the property. Lorraine and I figured the larger cabin would cut down on trips to the convenience store. It would also make it possible for us to stay longer and open the opportunity for wintertime visits.

Once the cabin was built, we gradually made improvements as time allowed. We screened-in the front porch facing the pond and wired lights on the trees to illuminate the path leading to the fire pit. Eventually we added a dock and other amenities for the lake. Everyone pitched in and donated unneeded furniture and cookware. The cabinets were filled with board games, dominoes, and roasting sticks. This cabin ended up being called the "Lake House" to differentiate it from the older green cabin by the county road.

The inside of the Lake House became filled with memories. Walking down from the second floor, where everyone slept, one saw a mirror that belonged to my great-grandmother. An old saw used by ancestors hung above the couch below a piece of sealed West Texas Mesquite with Romans 10:13 carved in the wood. Next to the bookcase was a frame holding a picture of Dad from his days in the navy, along with an envelope addressed to Delores Blake, my mother.

For the family, the farm provided something all families need. It helped Lorraine, Dwayne, Dad, and I remember times without pain and sickness. The family land helped preserve and strengthen our relationships with one another. Like a rock wall, the memories and time spent together served as stones hewn together to keep our family close. It served as a place to remember our own childhoods as we watched our children and grandchildren create similar memories on the same tract of land, climbing the same trees, wading in the same crawfish holes, and fishing the same tanks.

In a photo album at my daughter Emily's home, you'll find a picture of a blond-haired girl sporting a Safeway cap while holding a fishing pole. That girl is Emily. The picture captured a moment in time two decades ago, but the picture somehow came back to life as our blond-haired granddaughter, Ellie, stood on the dock looking into the same pond, sporting a pink camouflaged cap, and hoping for a fish to get on her line even if she had no intention of touching the slimy crappie.

* * * *

Mama endured her treatments with all the class we loved her for, but eventually the treatments stopped. It became apparent the end of her life was near. God had indeed given us more time. Instead of three months from September 10, 2001, we enjoyed three years.

All of the family made plans to visit Mama at her hospice care center in Rowlett, Texas. Nancy took off from work for the last couple of weeks of my mother's life to care for Mama day and night.

On the weekend before Mama went to be with the Lord, Nancy, my daughters, their husbands, and I stood around Mama as she mostly kept her eyes closed. Everyone expressed their love and took turns saying good-bye. Dad walked into the room, and I witnessed what happens when a man's heart mourns for his wife. He looked at Mama, and she looked at him. Tears brimmed in his eyes. The sadness of eventual loss broke my strong, determined dad. He turned and walked out of the room.

My mother cried as I tried to assure her that her husband of fifty-two years would get better. "We'll take care of him," I promised.

Mama and I prayed for God to take her home. Shortly after the prayer, my mother looked in my direction with weariness in her eyes. "Dale Richard," she whispered. "Take care of your dad and your sister. I love you."

She didn't say much else. We witnessed her last breath on November 15, 2004. God, in His mercy, gave us all more time than we had expected. We turned our attention to her funeral and the contacting of friends and relatives. After the visitation, Dwayne and his family, Lorraine and her family, and my family met up at Braum's for ice cream. We all laughed and shared stories. The laughter brought sorely needed emotional fresh air. I believe the scene must have brought a smile to Mama's heavenly face.

The funeral for Mama, who was always a bright and fun

person, came on a cold, rainy day. My mother's minister preached, read Scripture, and described a generous life. He told how Mama volunteered around the church, provided scholarships for kids to go to camp, and sold chocolate chip cookies to raise funds for a water well in India.

My brother-in-law, Keith, made a slide show of pictures that played during the service. I had always enjoyed slide shows, but the pictures for this one drew a wide range of responses. Some pictures drew laughter, while others encouraged tears. Dad reached his hand toward the screen and cried, "Mama."

Not long after the funeral, around Thanksgiving, the family gathered at a familiar place – the farm. After unloading bags and food, the guys built a campfire in the pit. We all gathered around the fire as the stars came out. The coyotes howled, and the notorious pump jack thumped. On future trips to the farm, I would convince my grandchildren the noise came from Indians beating drums. I had told my children the same story twenty years earlier. I sensed a therapeutic quality in the time spent together. A great depth of collective water had passed under life's bridge for all of us, but the time around the campfire provided an opportunity to bask in the blessing of God, demonstrated in creation and in those we love.

My mother's bout with cancer had shaken some rocks from the family wall. Every family experiences similar difficulties in life. Someone has to come in and encourage people to clear the rubble and rebuild. It takes determination and resolve to believe that what an illness or difficulty tore down is worth rebuilding.

In the Old Testament, the Israelites struggled to rebuild the temple and city walls after the Babylonians destroyed the Holy City's iconic structures. Leaders and prophets like Ezra, Zerubbabel, Haggai, Nehemiah, and Zechariah led the people to bring new life to Jerusalem. The reconstruction effort brought new optimism and healing for the people in Jerusalem.

Moments like the one around the campfire gave my family the time and space to create moments to rebuild the valuable-but-fragmented pieces of our lives. In similar fashion to replacing rocks from the temple's wall, rebuilding the family wall is critical because one never knows when the next attack might come.

3

THE MORRISON HUDDLE

Nancy prepared diligently for Courtney's birth. All nursery items were organized in their proper place. We welcomed Courtney into the world on March 4, 1981. Our second daughter, Emily, followed just over one year later when Nancy delivered her on August 9, 1982. I find dates fascinating in the way they connect. For instance, my youngest daughter, Malory, would marry her husband thirty years and one day after Courtney was born.

A child's birth is always a happy occasion. When it is your own child, the exhilaration skyrockets. From observing our daughters' arrivals, I knew that as exciting as it was to welcome a new life into the world, the experience was especially tiring for mothers. The pushing, the breathing, and the hours of labor all deplete the mother's strength.

Nancy experienced a significant reduction in sleep. With all of the buildup to a baby's birthday, I found myself admiring how everyone knew what to do when the baby arrived. The doctor knew to suction the baby's airways and to prepare the umbilical cord for cutting, while the nurses knew to check the baby's vitals and examine for possible health issues. I am proud of Malory as she fulfills this important role as a labor and delivery nurse.

Early into our marriage, Nancy and I enjoyed the blessing of two children, and then discovered she was pregnant
with our third child. We circled the due date on our calendar.
Nancy carried our third baby while trying to keep up with two
preschool-age children. When we neared the third trimester,
the child died. We no longer wondered whether it was a boy
or girl, or what it would look like, or how big he or she would
be. Those questions expired and gave way to new questions.

There was no bundle of joy for us to hold after nine months.
What role do you fill when a baby dies? What do you do when
there is no cord to be cut, no ears to be cleaned, and no nose
to be suctioned? The roles Nancy and I expected to fulfill felt
cruelly stolen. The worst part was wondering how a beautiful
story of life might have unfolded.

* * * *

After Mama's service to celebrate her life, my family and I drove
to my childhood home on Maple Drive. An incredible sadness
washed over me as I faced new realities. Mama wouldn't be
here to make me feel at home. Never again would she make an
egg-custard pie for me. Never again would I hear her say, "I
love you, Dale Richard."

When I walked through the door, I headed straight to the
back of the house to an empty bedroom. I shut the door, collapsed on the bed, and took a moment to pray specifically for
strength. I expressed gratefulness to the Lord for my mother's
life, her warmth, and the way she loved her family. Mama always
encouraged me to do well and to treat other people right. She
often emphasized the teaching of Luke 6:31: *And as ye would
that men should do to you, do ye also to them likewise.* In other
words, love others the way you would have them love you.
Respect others in the way you would have them respect you.

I learned generosity from my mother. The fruit of the Spirit as described in Galatians, including love, joy, and peace, was completely evident in her life.

Growing up on Maple Drive in Garland provided for a wonderful childhood. My dad worked for Safeway as a truck driver, and my mom stayed at home to raise three children. We had a special home, celebrated wonderful holidays, and never doubted the love my parents had for us.

My parents faithfully took us to church. Dad drove the church bus through the neighborhoods picking up children for Sunday school and church services. Like all kids, I daydreamed and thought about playing baseball and football with friends, during some church services; but for the most part, I looked forward to going to church as a family. And when we weren't at church, my parents lived the gospel.

When I was young, my childhood obsessions normally included anything to do with a ball and exercising an entrepreneurial spirit. My first love was for baseball. I earned All-Star honors every year. In my junior high and high school years, I turned to football, the unofficial state sport of Texas.

If Texas were to become its own country again, it might be tempted to celebrate New Year's Eve on the first night of Friday football. People in Texas are extremely passionate about high school football, the Dallas Cowboys, and their favorite college teams. Football is so much a part of life in America that sociologists use the term "huddle" to describe family dynamics.

Naturally, as a Texan born boy, I thought about football with every breath. I experienced above-average success on the gridiron. I received recruitment letters from several college coaches, including one from Darrell K. Royal, the legendary head coach from the University of Texas.

During my junior season, I received an invitation to work out with Dallas Cowboys' quarterback Roger Staubach. He hoped

I might consider going to the United States Naval Academy to play football. He also invited me to attend a Cowboys game at the old Texas Stadium with his wife, Marianne, and five children. It was my first time to see inside the hallowed grounds with the hole in the roof. I was told the hole was included in the stadium design so God could look down on His favorite team. I remember thinking, "Can't God see through a roof?" The whole experience with the famous quarterback and his family was an unforgettable afternoon.

Football gave me the opportunity to compete, which I loved, and to hit, which I loved even more. I loved to hit, make tackles, and punish the offensive player with the ball. One Friday night my team, the North Garland Raiders, prepared to face a tough rivalry. An article in the paper about the game highlighted the expected matchup of the rival's talented offensive lineman and me.

Upon reading the article, I thought of a way to get into the lineman's head. I didn't even reveal to my head coach what I prepared to do. I lined up on defense for the first play from scrimmage right across from my opponent. Before the quarterback snapped the ball, I exploded out of my stance into the lineman's numbers, knocking him on his back. My team went wild, and the lineman let me know his displeasure as well. In today's football, the referee would have flagged me for unsportsmanlike conduct, but football was a different game in the late 1970s. I managed to escape the play with only a five-yard encroachment penalty.

Football also presented me with the opportunity to be a leader. Before my senior year, my teammates voted me team captain. I approached the honor with complete devotion and enthusiasm. I encouraged my teammates to practice hard and play hard, implementing a lead-by-example policy. It was more than that though. God was working in my life to provide spiritual leadership for the team. I invited teammates to Young Life and Fellowship of Christian Athletes (FCA) meetings.

The day before the game on Friday, I invited one of my teammates, Jackie Smith, to go to Young Life with me. He came and seemed to enjoy the meeting. After Young Life was over, I said, "Jackie, I would like for you to come with me to FCA in the morning before school." He agreed. It thrilled me when he agreed to come. God had definitely placed Jackie on my heart.

When he walked into the FCA room the next morning, I prayed that the message from the Bible study would specifically speak to my teammate. After FCA, my teammates and I went about the day trying to focus on our assignments, when all we could really think about was X's and O's and how to win the game that night.

I can't remember much about the game that night except that we lost. After the game, the team showered and loaded the bus. Jackie happened to sit next to me on the bus. He was crying. Thinking he might be upset about the game, I tried to encourage him. Everyone had played hard, and I let him know he played a good game.

He said, "Dale, that's not it."

"Alright, what's bothering you?" I asked.

His next words have stayed with me for the last forty years. "I want to ask Christ to be my Lord and Savior."

We talked a few minutes about what our Young Life leaders and FCA leaders had talked to us about earlier that morning and the night before. Then Jackie prayed to God about his life, his sin, and his need of God's forgiveness.

When he finished his prayer of repentance and confession, more joy and adrenaline filled me than I'd ever experienced at any football game. I stood and got the attention of the rest of the team. I said, "Guys, we may have lost the game tonight and are down about that. But I have some great news. Jackie prayed a couple of minutes ago to trust Christ as his Savior."

For the first time that night, my teammates and I had a reason to cheer. My coach, Larry Beavers, wrote to me celebrating Jackie's decision. He wrote: "So glad we could share in the great experience like last Friday. Let's both pray that God will continue to use us and that we will be available to him."

Football season ended and the rest of my senior year consisted of two objectives – to finish school and try to get along with my father. Due to our mutual stubbornness, we often butted heads. Our inability to get on the same page led to me leaving home. I finished the school year of 1977 while living with extended family members.

I wanted to play football in college and decided to move to Abilene, Texas, to play for the McMurry Indians (now the McMurry War Hawks).

Football at McMurry was similar to football at North Garland High School, but the game was faster and harder hitting. I enjoyed the fall football season and prepared for the final game of the year. In the course of the game, I hit the running back, causing him to fumble the ball. I grabbed the ball before an offensive player could recover. The exciting play drew a loud, familiar whistle from the stands. From the shrillness of the whistle, I knew my dad was cheering me from the bleachers. His presence at the game meant a great deal and began to heal our relationship.

I played one season at McMurry and appreciated new friendships and the support it created in moving to a new town, but I also learned quickly that I wasn't going to head to the National Football League after McMurry. I needed a new direction in life.

I lived off campus, drove a red '62 Chevy Impala, and bought an old house even though I had very little money. The payment was $157 per month. With a car and a house payment, cash flow tightened. I didn't even have money to buy toilet paper. Since toilet paper is an essential part of life, I came up with the brilliant idea to head to my old dorm on campus and take toilet paper from the public restroom.

I parked in front of the dorm, walked inside, and quickly headed to the bathroom hoping no one I knew would walk down the hall. After stuffing my jacket full of toilet paper rolls, I walked out of the bathroom. Not five feet from the door, the residence hall director eyed me with a curious expression.

In a kind but inquisitive tone he asked, "What are you doing?"

I looked at the floor, looked back at him, and said, "I don't have the money to buy toilet paper." It's humorous now, but at the time it embarrassed me tremendously.

Graciously, he let me escape with one toilet paper roll. I had gone from a proud football player to a toilet paper thief in a very short time.

My dad's parting advice before I left Garland was to find a good church and a State Farm agent. I took his advice and did both. Other than that, I know I went to class in college, but I remember very little about the educational aspect of my higher education. Most of my memories involve football and school dances. I enjoyed campus socials and dancing to music from records like Kool and the Gang, Chicago, and the Eagles.

One dance changed my life forever. I walked into the dance without a date after a sports banquet, mingled a bit, and quickly noticed a young lady dancing. She wore a blue dress, and I knew I had to dance with her. At the time, she was dancing with a friend of mine – not my best friend, but a friend. I quickly devised the perfect plan to meet the girl and get my friend out of the picture. I walked up to them on the dance floor, tapped my friend on the shoulder, and told him a call had come for him on the payphone downstairs. He left the dance, and I happily took his place.

In the time my friend was gone, I introduced myself to an Abilene Christian University student named Nancy Stevens. I enjoyed the dance and felt it would lead to something more. My friend returned complaining that no one had called for him. I assured him that the call must have been accidently disconnected.

The semester soon ended, and my friend returned home to Waco for the summer. I remained in Abilene, which gave me time with Nancy while her boyfriend was out of the picture. To make sure it wouldn't hurt his feelings if I took Nancy on a few dates, I called him. To my surprise he agreed, but said, "Just one date. She is a special girl, and I would like to see her next fall." What neither of us realized at the time was that he had gone on his last date with Nancy Stevens.

On June 16, 1979, Nancy and I married and started our little huddle of a family. We soon welcomed a daughter named Courtney, and seventeen months later our second daughter, Emily. Our growing family lived in the small house until a couple of years after Emily's birth. I was climbing the ladder at work, and our Morrison family was doing quite well.

Before Courtney's arrival, I had started a job at Bank of Commerce in Abilene due to the recommendation of longtime friend and fellow McMurry student, Wayne Robertson. My first job at the bank was to recover property and possessions due to delinquency. I became a repo man, and I enjoyed the adrenaline rush associated with the job. I carried this tough-guy mentality with me, and I have to admit I relished the occasional fight.

Wayne eventually left the Bank of Commerce for a competitor bank in town and recruited me to join forces with him at First State Bank as head of collections. I worked in this position for less than two years before being promoted to the note department. From there, I secured a vice-president position in the loan department at twenty-five years old.

The promotion to vice president meant better pay and a desk. I drove to work filled with tremendous enthusiasm on my first day as a loan officer, wanting to make a strong impression with the senior officers and customers. I felt confident I could do an above-average job for First State Bank.

I perched myself on the corner of my desk to wait for a customer. Before the doors opened, my phone rang. The receptionist from across the bank advised me that I had left my zipper down and should probably resolve the issue before customers arrived. The lapse served as a lesson in humility.

When I started in the new position, our family of four lived in the house I had bought while in college. Nancy and I decided we had outgrown the two-bedroom house and wanted to find a piece of land in the country to build a new home.

While driving along county roads looking for the right place, Courtney, two years old at the time, announced, "I've got to go potty!" I quickly pulled over and led Courtney well off the road to avoid the possibility of the occasional car invading her privacy. As things wound down, I spotted a "for sale" sign lying in a patch of tall grass. It wasn't even visible from the road. I looked to the east and glimpsed the perfect hilltop to build on. I called the number on the sign and agreed to a deal.

We built a house, and it is our home to this day. As I evaluated life, I reflected on our progress. We had a beautiful home on a hill between Tuscola and Abilene. The bank business was going well. What more could a young man with a family expect?

After several successful years at First State Bank, Nancy and I anticipated the birth of our third child. We had two beautiful daughters and wondered if the third child would be a boy. I had originally planned, like most dads, to coach my son's football or baseball team, but with two girls, I had to switch those plans to girls' basketball. The switch didn't bother me. When the girls were old enough to play, I coached their team with the same intensity I'd have displayed if coaching a group of boys.

During the sixth month of the pregnancy, one evening Nancy looked at me with a hint of concern in her eyes. "I think something might be wrong with the baby." We wasted no time and scheduled an appointment. Nancy's doctor confirmed our worst fears as he performed a sonogram. Our third child had died in the womb. The news was devastating.

We named the baby D.N. Morrison for Dale and Nancy and decided not to learn our baby's gender. I built a small wooden casket and Nancy made a hand-embroidered pillow to place inside it. Our pastor, Elbert Peak, and his wife met us at the cemetery to mourn and pray with us.

Soon after we buried our third child, Nancy and I encountered further turbulence. This time the source was my job as vice president at First State Bank. For some time, I discerned the Lord prompting me to resign from my position. The bank, due to unethical management and a retreating economy in the early 1980's, teetered on the brink of collapse. The dependable paycheck and nice position made it difficult to jump ship even though the signs of failure were all around me.

The decision was made for me as tension between myself and a higher-ranking bank official led to my forced resignation. In hindsight, what I interpreted then as a cruel act to fire me, only one week after burying my child, turned out to be a blessing when not long after that the bank closed its doors.

God definitely had my attention. A lost job and a lost child in the same week brought incredible sadness and stress to our home. God had given me a family to take care of. I tried to examine my life to see if maybe I wasn't doing everything I should be doing as a Christian father and husband. I prayed more, read my Bible more, and went to church more.

My prayer life deepened in a new way. It grew beyond

prayers before meals or at church. I sought times with God to discern what He wanted for my marriage and my children. Prayer brought answers and solutions, which led to changes in my home. I pinpoint this time in my life as a God-given opportunity to renew my walk with Jesus and place a refreshed emphasis upon learning what it meant to be a godly husband, father, and friend.

I also looked outside myself to focus on the needs of my family and of boys who needed a Christian role model. I decided since I had no boys to play football with, I would find a boys' team that needed a coach. The Pop Warner football program in Abilene was the perfect place for this to happen. The league assigned me the Giants. I would coach the same group of boys for the next four years.

I tried to interact with the boys like Coach Beavers had done back when I played at North Garland High School. I looked up to him as a great mentor to follow, for he had demonstrated the gifts of leadership and coaching. If I could lead like my high school coach, I'd make a difference in the lives of these young boys while we enjoyed learning the game.

The Giants performed well, and the team made it all the way to the Pop Warner Abilene Championship. In one of our championship games, we played an opponent from the wealthier side of town. The Giants were from the north side and our opponent from the south side. The south side had a mall and fancy restaurants. The north side featured hamburger stands and thrift stores. It turned into a North-versus-South civil war.

The town really got into the game, and I gave a quote to the newspaper guaranteeing a victory for the Giants. The day of the game came, and after a tough first half, we entered halftime down seven points. During halftime, the opposing team flaunted their team's money by changing into fresh, clean jerseys. Our boys were fortunate to have one jersey. I used this football field fashion display to motivate our team and led them onto the field for the second half. I told the Giants, "This team thinks they are better than you in every way. Prove them wrong."

Our team fought hard and was in position to win the game. We had taken the lead when the other team started to drive the ball on the last possession of the game. In the last few seconds of the fourth quarter, a defender for the Giants intercepted a pass to secure victory. I have never been more proud of a football team than I was of the scrappy Pop Warner Giants.

Another highlight with the Giants was a young boy named Paul Watts who is now a doctor. He secured a position on the Giants as field goal kicker. A situation presented itself where we could attempt a long field goal or go for it on fourth down. I signaled for a time-out and brought the team over to the sidelines.

Not very many teams of twelve-year-olds kick extra points, much less a long field goal, but I believed Paul had the leg to kick that distance successfully. In the huddle, I spoke to our kicker: "Paul, how would you like to make a twenty-eight-yard field goal?" I looked him in the eye. "You can make this field goal," I said. He nodded and agreed that he could do it.

I sent the team out to the field to line up in field goal formation. A hush fell across the stands. I'm sure parents questioned my strategy, and the butterflies in my gut were greater than anything I had ever experienced as a Raider for North Garland.

Our center snapped the ball. The hold was good. Paul kicked the ball. For a moment, it seemed like a dream; the ball sailed through the uprights for a last-second field goal to win the game. I will never forget the memories made with those boys. Coaching football was an avenue to encourage young men and to work through my loss and my sadness.

After D.N.'s burial, I also felt compelled to do more as a family. Nancy and I didn't have much when we married, causing us to work extra hours and extra jobs to provide for our family, but we also needed to enjoy time as a family huddle. We came up with the slogan "Work Hard, Play Hard" with our girls. Nancy and I had gone to South Padre on our honeymoon and decided to return to the beach with Courtney and Emily.

We also made it a priority to attend church in a disciplined manner. Devoting time for worship, teaching, and discipleship proved to be a new blessing for Nancy and me. My faith grew significantly, and the Lord used all of this as a healing salve to our sadness and stress.

After leaving First State Bank, I performed consultant work for two banks. My main responsibility was to solve difficult-to-resolve problems. I would be the "decider." The experience as a consultant led to a vice-president position at Winters State Bank with Bobby Airhart. The new job provided further stability for our family.

After half a decade in our new home and a new job, on February 2, 1988, God blessed us with our third daughter, Malory. She sported a full head of black hair, and her two big sisters were eager to help Nancy with the baby. Her birth brought even more closure to losing D.N. My family seemed complete.

After managing loan accounts at Winters State Bank for a couple of years, Nancy and I encountered a career challenge that far outweighed my previous loss of employment. Bobby and I were set to foreclose on an area rancher. Our actions initiated a legal process for the bank to acquire the ranch from the property owner. I knew the rancher would be furious, because most owners responded in anger when the bank foreclosed on their property. Much to everyone's shock, the rancher responded in a way Bobby and I had never experienced in our combined years of banking.

A Texas Ranger law enforcement investigation in conjunction with the FBI secured audio recordings of the cattleman/landowner from Coleman County attempting to hire a man to serve as a hitman to kill the bank's president and me. By God's grace, the man contacted by the landowner went to the authorities. The FBI and the Texas Rangers had the man return to the rancher to record incriminating evidence.

A Texas Ranger met with Bobby and me at the bank to let us hear the recordings. As the tape played, I heard this man plan my murder. The hitman was to pull me over between my house and the bank, pull me out of the car, and pour acid in my eyes. He was then to tie me up and throw me in a previously dug hole, burying me alive. The rancher also knew my wife's vehicle and the route she took to shuttle our children to and from school. *My family!* I feared for their safety.

After leaving the meeting, Bobby and I took immediate action to secure our families' safety. I called my father. He immediately left Garland to escort Nancy and the girls to school. Men from our church, led by Dan Whetzel, set a gate at the end of our road, and I had a security system installed at the house. The unfolding story reached the local media, and I couldn't go anywhere without someone asking me about the situation.

Authorities arrested the rancher a week later and a court date was set. Much to our dismay, the man only received five years' probation, and the court denied the foreclosure. The bank had to eat the loss, and a man who wanted to end my life in terrifying fashion walked free.

Eventually our fears related to the hit on my life calmed, but the anti-banking climate of the 1980s made it difficult to stay in banking. Even though I had a strong relationship with Bobby and a respect for the banking business, the economy and rulings against banks, like the one involving the Coleman County ranch, made it difficult for banks to succeed. My position at the bank went away. I had to look for something else to provide for my family. This time I wanted to take advantage of the new opportunity; I wanted to control my own destiny by being my own boss.

While trying to formulate plan B, I called a friend and coworker from First State Bank, Jerry Hallmark, to meet for lunch. He had recently lost his job too, when the bank closed its doors. Jerry and I had worked a few small investments together, but I hoped he would be interested in turning periodic dealings into a full-fledged business partnership.

I first met Jerry under less-than-desirable circumstances. I had borrowed a First State Bank car while taking documents between the various bank branches around town, when another vehicle struck me. The accident wasn't my fault, but I had to report it. I was worried the bank might reprimand me or fire me. The report of the accident took place in Jerry's office. He responded graciously and said, "Cars are replaceable, but people are not. I am glad you are okay."

As Jerry and I sat down to discuss future opportunities, I felt a similar uncertainty. However, the second meeting ended as positively as the first. Jerry agreed to explore new business opportunities together. I had taken the plunge from a steady paycheck to the frontier of self-employment.

Nancy and I spent the next few months figuring out how to make my new work venture mesh with our financial obligations. As I figured things out in my new partnership, we enjoyed watching our daughters grow from little girls to young ladies. This brought equal measures of blessing and frustration. Nancy and I committed ourselves to provide a godly, safe home for our daughters. The way my parents raised me influenced my own parenting style. To give you an idea of where I was coming from, here is a saying my dad wrote for our church's letter printed for Father's Day 1976: "Anyone can become a father. It's what the children become that counts."

One at a time, Courtney, Emily, and Malory prayed to receive

Christ as their Savior. Each experience was special and unique. Courtney prayed to receive Christ at a youth group Disciple Now event. Emily believed in Jesus Christ in our living room. Malory prayed at the altar of Gateway Baptist Church for Jesus to enter her life as Lord and Savior. Ingrained in a pile of special memories is Malory's first step from our family's pew to pray at the altar with her mother and me. The girls had a love for God and their family, but they also did things that tested their parents' patience.

Like many dads, I'd come home after a long day of working on the rig or driving a backhoe and Nancy would greet me with an assignment – spank one of the girls for something they'd done during the day. If one of them acted up severely, they spent the next day at a location picking up rocks and trash or hoeing weeds in the vegetable garden. The plan was to use the day as punishment and for character building, but the time together normally transitioned into a special father/daughter day.

As our three girls got older, I tried to schedule regular one-on-one dates with each of them. We'd go eat a meal, share ice cream, or get a coke together. I'd use the time to hear about school, friends, and challenges they faced. The special times gave them my complete attention and let them know how much I loved them. I often asked how I could make things better for them. Today, I am grateful for how my three girls kept their faith in Christ all through school, honored their mother and father, and worked hard.

When it came time for each daughter to graduate from high school and go to college, we had a special meal and family gathering to recognize their accomplishment. We considered this milestone a major life transition for the girls but also for Nancy and me. Going to college and graduating from college meant more than leaving home. It also meant new young men coming into our family.

Being a young man once myself, I knew what I desired their dating life to be and what I wanted it not to be. Courtney brought home Phil, Emily brought home Jacob, and Malory brought home Steve. With all three men, I took time to sit down with them and ask questions to get to know them and learn about their backgrounds. If you ask Phil, I cooked him well done and I slightly toasted the others during the interviews.

A man didn't date our daughters without getting to know me first. When Jacob initially wanted to date Emily, she informed him that he would have to meet with me first, then Emily set up the opportunity for us all to meet.

Emily and Jacob drove to our home a few miles south of Abilene. They turned off the highway onto a paved county road. After a few miles, they turned onto a private drive making a slow climb to the top of the hill. I hoped that he'd grow more nervous with every quarter mile.

I looked out the window as they pulled up. Emily and Jacob chatted nervously as they climbed from Jacob's pickup. Maybe she offered up final preparations. She had witnessed Courtney's anxiety when I grilled her future husband. Phil confidently states that his interview was by far more challenging than any that followed, and claims that I ran a much tighter ship over Phil and Courtney's courtship. I don't fully agree with him, but he's welcome to his opinion.

Nancy accessed available sources and had some information on the young man coming to meet us. He grew up in Sonora. I had heard of Sonora due to the popularity of the Caverns of Sonora. Nancy also discovered he had good grades and was a Bible major. Emily also tried to sell me on how she met this nice guy in her critical thinking class at Hardin-Simmons University. She had struggled with some homework, and he willingly helped her learn the complicated issues related to writing arguments and uncovering fallacies.

Emily opened the door and everyone clustered around to get a glimpse of the new guy in my daughter's life. First, Malory walked towards the door with an enthusiastic smile. Then Nancy headed to the entryway, and finally I made my way to the door. Having gotten in from a day of moving dirt, I chose to be comfortable for our first meeting and dressed in my best pajama pants. After a few minutes of introduction, all of the ladies walked to the back part of the house as if on cue.

Jacob joined me at the dining table while I finished a left-over steak. Between bites, I asked about his parents, family, and home life. The questions around the table were soft tosses that gave him a chance to warm up for the fastballs to come. After I finished the steak, we moved to the living room. The move was one of location but also of intensity.

Sitting in the living room, I asked Jacob about his faith. He shared that he accepted Christ at age nine and was pursuing a ministry degree in college. I asked him about previous dating relationships. He had little to report. I moved on to what he planned to do while dating my daughter. After his response, I laid out some intentional ground rules.

In essence, I wanted Jacob to move slowly, very slowly. The conditions weren't impossible, and he felt fine with those rules. The interview ended with a manly side hug. For now, he had passed the test. If he only knew, it was the first of many to come.

One way I test a man is by taking him to work. The type of work I do and ask others to do is not easy. The crews for Jerry and I work long summer hours, and they sweat profusely raking out dirt to remove all the clods before hydro-mulching a yard.

While enjoying a meal a couple of weeks later with Emily and her new boyfriend, I mentioned I needed someone at the end of the day on my crew. By four o'clock, the men started to tire, and I wanted a set of fresh arms and legs to wrap up the day. Having myself been a poor college student who stole toilet paper, I knew Jacob could use the money.

All of what I told Jacob about needing assistance was entirely true, but I had additional motives. After placing a rake in Jacob's hand, I had a firsthand opportunity to review his work ethic and willingness to receive instruction. In spite of blisters and extremely sore muscles, he returned the next day still wanting to make a good impression and to be the kind of man I would want for my daughter.

Wedding days as a dad to three girls meant being tossed into an emotional blender. Let me start with a positive emotions. Pride welled up within me to be the one privileged to walk Courtney, Emily, and Malory down the wedding aisle. I had held their hands as they learned to walk. I swatted their bottoms when they learned to talk back. I took my girls with me to check on oil wells and gardens. My little girls had grown into beautiful, God-honoring women. The hard part was giving up the place of "most-loved man" in their lives. Later, on special days like Valentine's Day, I would say to them, "Remember girls, I was your first Valentine."

Every time I waited for the doors to open at Logsdon Chapel on the campus of Hardin-Simmons University in Abilene, I wanted to make sure I said the right words at the right time, but I also wanted to grasp God's blessing as the family huddle expanded before my eyes. With each marriage came a new son-in-law and later, grandchildren. Knowing all that I had lost and all that I had received, I sought to express gratitude every day for all the Lord had bestowed on me through my huddle with Nancy, my daughters, and their families.

4

TO THE ENDS OF THE EARTH

I sat in the backseat gazing out of my window at the mosaic of people walking the streets and riding rickshaws. Mopeds holding up to three passengers weaved in and out of marked traffic lanes that seemed to be nothing more than mere decoration. Suffice it to say that traffic lanes in Bangalore, India, and a toothpick for a toothless mouth serve a similar uselessness.

Our reasonable mode of transportation came to stop at a light on the crowded street. I could have easily rolled down my window and shook the hand of the moped rider next to us. All the images of India's overcrowded city streets fail to depict the reality of the swarm cramming the roadways. For the first few hours, you feel as if the entire billion-plus population might fall on top of you. I recalled the words of Jesus in Acts and wondered, "Lord, is this what the ends of the earth look like?"

The sights and sounds of Bangalore, the capital of Karnataka, overwhelmed my senses. Jay Capra sat in the front seat. In the seat across from me sat longtime friend Abraham Bhasme. He looked right at home on his city's streets, while I surely must have looked slightly anxious as I gripped the door handle. As a normally confident person, at this moment I felt vulnerable. But even with this sense of unease, I had no doubt I was where

I needed to be. I knew the Lord had a plan and a significant reason for why my path crossed with Brother Bhasme.

My name for Abraham is Brother Abraham. Brother Abraham was a servant. He was an evangelist, a stirring preacher, a visionary, and a sensible leader. The first time we met was one of the best, unexpected chance meetings in my life. Brother Abraham found me. I clearly didn't find him. The fact that he ended up in Abilene, Texas, all the way from Bangalore, in our church, is a gift from God in my life and my family's life.

* * * *

In 1989, when my youngest daughter, Malory, hadn't yet reached the terrible two's, my family did what we always did the night of the midweek church service – we went to church. Rarely did anything out of the norm happen when we gathered on those nights, but on this particular night, that was about to change. This midweek service exceeded my highest expectations.

Our pastor was out of town that night, but days before he left, he had received a phone call from a native pastor from India. Brother Abraham had, in faith, arranged for a one-way plane ticket from India to the Dallas-Fort Worth airport. He arrived in Dallas, caught a bus to Abilene, and used the bus station pay phone to call local churches looking for a place to speak and share his ministry and burden for India.

Brother Abraham had little money for the calls, and after struggling to actually get through to any of the pastors in town, he called the Big Country Baptist Church and talked with our pastor. After a short visit to hear about his faith and doctrinal beliefs, the pastor invited Brother Abraham to preach in his absence for the upcoming midweek service, and to use the time to tell the people about his ministry to the vast nation of India. He also promised Brother Abraham that he could sleep on the floor in the church nursery that night. As uncomfortable as that might be, at least he had a place to lay his head and overcome jet lag.

I didn't know anything about these arrangements until I arrived at the church for the usual Bible study and prayer service. When I discovered a guest from India would speak, I grew eager to hear about his ministry.

From the pulpit, a church member introduced Brother Abraham. Our guest rose from his seat and walked to the platform. He stood tall, sported a mustache, and had an amiable presence.

Our guest preached a great message and the service concluded with an offering for his ministry. As a part of his message, Brother Abraham made an appeal for pastors in India. He hoped to raise funds while in America so the pastors could have bikes to ride while visiting in rural villages. I didn't know much about ministers in India, but I thought they were sure to have skinnier waistlines than American pastors. Outside of Mormon missionaries, I had never seen a pastor make use of a bike in his visitation.

After the service, I walked to the front of the church to meet my only connection to India. While introducing myself to Brother Abraham, I learned he didn't have a hotel room but planned to sleep in the nursery. Not wanting him to sleep on a nursery floor, I invited him to our home. My daughters still remind me of how significant that night was in their lives. It was impossible to know the depth of impact it would have on my young family.

Our guest for the night loaded his bag into our suburban for the short drive home. We pulled up to the house and I tapped the button for the garage door to rise. My new friend from India quickly jerked up in his seat with an incredulous look. He had never seen an automatic garage door.

"Where are your servants, brother? How did the door rise?" His question caused our girls to giggle.

We sat around and talked for about an hour, and I knew he must have been exhausted. I encouraged our guest to get some rest. We had a great bed in our guest room, and I promised him a good night's sleep. We all went to our bedrooms.

The following morning, Brother Abraham and I made small talk during breakfast.

"How was the bed last night?" I asked.

"Oh brother, I guess it would have been fine, but I grabbed a pillow and slept on the floor. The beds in America are too soft."

Once I knew he had slept on the floor, I realized the church nursery room accommodations weren't an insult after all.

Brother Abraham stayed several nights in our house, and my family grew to love him tremendously. He endeared himself to our girls, graciously received our hospitality, and offered advice when our ways as a culture differed significantly from the way of life in India. Our movies, musical lyrics, and nation's sexual overdrive troubled him greatly. He also felt strongly that our worship services failed to honor the Word of God appropriately.

That first visit launched a rapport that spanned two decades. I compare the relationship I had with Brother Abraham to the relationship the Apostle Paul must have had with young Timothy. The gentle pastor from Bangalore became a mentor. Throughout our friendship, he demonstrated a willingness to be a man with whom I could share burdens, prayer requests, and dreams. We talked Scripture and devoted hours to studying the Bible together.

After returning to Bangalore, Brother Abraham knew he had a friend in Abilene and vice versa. Our friendship and interest in India led me to arrange plans for a mission trip to India. This allowed me to learn more about Brother Abraham's ministry and to have the opportunity to be a witness to the ends of the earth. I wanted to do all I could to support his ministry, which included Victory Baptist Bible College, a children's home, and seventy-two churches and pastors.

* * * *

Fifteen years later, in March of 2004, I sat next to Brother Abraham in India's multi-directional traffic with my best friend, Dr. Jay Capra, a pediatrician in Abilene, riding in the front seat. Our families attended the same church.

We finally arrived at Brother Abraham's home. I noticed a water tower on top of the house as I climbed out of the vehicle to meet the rest of the Bhasme family. I had met his wife in a previous visit to our home, but I only knew stories about his four children.

A big family greeted Jay and me as we walked into the Bhasme living room. The aroma of curry wafted in to the modestly decorated room. I thought about washing up before dinner, but I knew the water tower I'd seen stored water for home use because water only flowed to the house at a certain time of day. Brother Abraham introduced us to his wife, Selina, his sons, Stanley and Joshua, and his two daughters, Salome and Joyce. A connection with his family formed instantaneously.

After meeting and greeting the family, I anticipated the flavors of Indian cuisine waiting for us at the Bhasmes' dining table. In the times my Bangalore friend had visited America, he cooked traditional Indian recipes that our family loved. The aroma of peanut rice and curry chicken filled the room.

Before the meal, as head of the Bhasme family, Brother Abraham offered a blessing. He stood as a proud father, and I felt honored to become acquainted with a family that had a long legacy of serving Christ in Bangalore and southern India. Brother Abraham's father had served in Christian vocation

as well as his grandfather. His grandfather had the distinc-
tion of translating the Hebrew Bible into the native language
of Bangalore. I considered the family seated around the table.
The future of the family's ministry sat in the room also. His
two sons would one day go on with the ministry with the hope
that their children would also carry on the family ministry.

While in India, our feet never grew comfortable with the
ground on which they stood. Our pastor and guide kept us
moving. After traveling with Brother Abraham by train to
meet with the many churches and pastors under his care and
direction, Jay and I felt humbled by their commitment and
dedication to pastoring and building up the body of Christ.
They met in huts and unfinished concrete structures. The
members walked long distances, and upon their arrival sat on
the floor in sanctuaries, lacking the comforts Americans took
for granted. None of the inconveniences or sacrifices hindered
their eager worship of God.

My first experience in India humbled me in every way. Each
church demonstrated true hospitality with the little they had.
Brother Abraham had the respect of every pastor and church
family member. I admired his leadership.

The people in the churches demonstrated deep appreciation
for God's Word and wanted preachers to preach. Sermons lasted
much longer than at my home church. I witnessed the effective-
ness of the pastors in caring for their people and encouraging
them in their faith in Christ. No impact was greater than the
humble living conditions of the people. Their possessions and
wealth were minimal, but their joy and pleasure in God was
abundant.

My time in India also gave me the opportunity to learn more
about my spiritual mentor, Brother Abraham. I knew from
our time in Abilene that my friend was both a gentleman and
a scholar. He demonstrated a deep humility and appreciation

for everything my family tried to do for him. He also respected my family and me. You might describe his behavior as meek and soft spoken as long as he wasn't behind a pulpit. In the pulpit, I saw a confidence in God's Word expressed in every syllable of his sermon.

In India, I saw a different side of Brother Abraham. He demonstrated unquestionable strength and commitment to his dream. He clearly had the respect of his family, pastors, professors, and college students. What Brother Abraham said was the final word on every issue.

Jay and I concluded our trip and returned home eager to share with our churches and family how God had worked in our lives and how touched we were by Abraham's family and the believers in India. I knew every dollar raised in support of his ministry had real kingdom impact, and I knew God could use my church, my friends, and my family to sustain and grow Brother Abraham's ministry. I enlisted my brother-in-law, Keith, to assist in producing a video to show the next time Abraham visited supporting churches in America.

In the summer of 2005, Brother Abraham returned to Abilene. He and his wife, whom we call Mrs. Abraham, instead of Mrs. Bhasme, stayed at our home for a couple of months. I loved traveling with Brother Abraham to churches. His English had improved greatly in the fifteen years of our friendship, but his ability to stick with the allotted time given for his messages had not. He loved to preach, and I would have to hold my hand out in the aisle of the church and point at my watch repeatedly to let him know his time was up. I always regretted rushing him though. I could sit for hours to take in a message given by Brother Abraham.

His sermons made the most of every second allotted to him, and I enjoyed hearing his heart for the pastors within his ministry and for the people reached through the ministry. I loved the compassion he and his staff demonstrated to children through his children's home. I saw promise in the students trained at Victory Baptist Bible College. More than anything, I loved hearing him preach. I can still hear my friend saying, "If a baby is born in a bus, it doesn't make him a bus. If a baby is born in a Christian family, this doesn't make the baby a Christian. Each person has to decide on his own to follow Christ in faith."

During this visit, my daughter Emily drove him to First Baptist Church in Rotan. Nancy and I weren't able to go. Brother Abraham was to preach in the evening service, meet with the youth group, and prepare Indian food for the students. It had taken more time than expected to cook all of the food before they left our house to make the hour-long drive to Rotan and left them running significantly late for the service. Emily had also struggled to keep Brother Abraham from operating on Indian time. Emily felt compelled to drive well over the speed limit to make it to the service in time. Brother Abraham nervously looked at Emily and said, "Oh, sister! You're going fast! I'll pray!"

They made it to the church in time and had a wonderful experience. Brother Abraham preached a great message. The students gobbled up the food. After the meal, the teenagers enjoyed dialogue with the guest preacher and chef. One student made an odd request by asking him to sing the Indian national anthem, which he proudly performed for the students.

The church connected with Brother Abraham in such a powerful way that First Baptist Rotan's pastor, Corkey Wells, and his son Benjamin traveled to India the next spring for meetings in Hubli, Brother Abraham's hometown.

The closer I grew to the Indian minister the harder it was for us to part company. Brother Abraham had become a boundless source of spiritual encouragement, and he had an immense knowledge of the Bible. We would discuss Bible passages at great length. I knew he loved our family, and he knew we loved him and his family. The mentoring relationship is one the Lord used to grow and shape my life.

When it came time for our friend to return home, Nancy and I drove Brother Abraham to the airport, assisted in getting his luggage checked in, and gave him a hug before he went through security. Brother Abraham took a few steps towards the security line and stopped. He turned towards me and said, "If I don't see you again, I will see you in heaven." Without another word, he waved and walked through security.

I had plans to take a group the next spring to India, and I couldn't wait for that time to come. A large group had met with Brother Abraham while he was in Abilene, and the meeting generated an infectious enthusiasm for the trip. My wife, two of my daughters, one son-in-law, my sister, and her husband all planned to go. I couldn't wait for them to have the experience in India with Brother Abraham and his family that I had enjoyed the year before.

On November 12, 2005, almost a year after my mother's death, I received a phone call from Stanley, Abraham's son, with alarming news. His dad had suffered a heart attack and had made it to a Bangalore hospital alive. The doctor felt confident his condition was stable but wanted to keep him a few days. My children came to the house so we could call Brother Abraham in the hospital.

Everyone passed the phone around offering words of encouragement and assuring him of their prayers. My friend's voice sounded weaker than normal, but his tone was confident that everything would be fine. After a week's rest, he would return home to his normal activities.

The next morning, I received a phone call that Abraham had suffered a second heart attack that led to his death. The day proved very difficult for his immediate family, the association of churches, the children and students, and his adopted family from the United States. The day became even more troubling when Stanley's father-in-law also died just a couple of hours after his father Abraham had died.

With Brother Abraham's death, I lost a friend, mentor, and confidant. I owed a significant amount of spiritual growth to this man. Nancy and I did our best to express our sorrow to Mrs. Abraham, but part of me wondered if Brother Abraham knew something when he turned around in the security line in the Dallas airport to speak to me one last time before boarding.

Plans for the spring trip moved forward, but I knew the tone would change. Everyone in the group remained eager to share their faith at the evangelistic services, to love on the children at the children's home, and to celebrate with the Bible college graduates. In Brother Abraham's departure to eternity, the trip gained an additional purpose. God would use our group to love the Bhasme family after a sudden, unexpected loss of a father, husband, and visionary leader for the ministry of Christ.

In March 2006 our group left from the Dallas-Fort Worth Airport for the mission trip to India. Fifteen people arrived in Bangalore ready to see a completely new world. As is the case with most experiences in a new culture, India is like encountering a new, exotic food group. The way you travel, dress, eat, and relate in conversation is different. Even the way believers worship is different. The team learned to eat using their left hand and with the correct technique. They struggled to adjust to the smells and holes in the train's floor that served as a toilet. In spite of culture shock, the team determined to share Christ with those at the services and to love the people. We prayed, preached, and shared testimonies. In our first opportunity to see Mrs. Abraham since her husband's death the previous autumn, we also mourned with Mrs. Abraham and her family over their loss.

The trip started with a graduation celebration at the college. Following the celebration, we enjoyed a rice and chicken curry meal and then headed towards the train station to travel north to Hubli. The previous fall, Brother Abraham had shared his vision to complete the new church building in Hubli by the time we arrived in March. The church was close to completion and would be dedicated during our trip. In the days before the dedication, we planned to hold outdoor evangelistic services near the church building.

We arrived in Hubli, went straight to the church building, and found a mess. Dust, debris, and building supplies littered the inside of the church. Painters climbed wooden scaffolding as other laborers worked with tile. The dedication was scheduled to happen in a couple of days. From my perspective, I couldn't see how that would happen. Once the actual construction was finished, there was still plenty of work to do. Chairs, instruments, and the pulpit still had to be installed. Our new friends worked furiously to get the building dedication ready.

Jet lag caught up to our team members and we needed to rest. We had joined in the effort until we couldn't stay up any longer. Finally, as much as we didn't want to, we retired to the hotel while the college students, pastors, and laborers kept working.

The next morning, dressed for the Hubli church dedication, our team loaded up in vans. I hoped for the best and feared the worst. People had traveled from all over the state to attend the dedication. City officials and one state senator planned to attend. I hoped they wouldn't be disappointed.

When the van stopped at the church, I hurried ahead to see the condition of the church. I couldn't believe my eyes! Not one piece of trash was in sight. The painters completed all their work, the tile shined brilliantly, and the chairs were queued nicely. Those working must have stayed up day and night to have the church ready for this special event.

People started to file into the church. Such a crowd gathered that the service grew to standing-room only. The congregation worshiped. Local officials congratulated the church on its accomplishment. Joshua and Stanley, Brother Abraham's sons, thanked everyone for contributions made in order for the dedication to be a success. The service couldn't have gone better.

The outstanding ceremony demonstrated that God's plan for Brother Abraham's ministry was ongoing – he had run the race and now the baton had been passed on to his children. It also allowed his family to heal from their loss and to express joy that this dream of Abraham's was fulfilled. He had always wanted a nice church structure in his hometown of Hubli. The new building stood majestically before us. As joyous as the occasion proved to be, it also held a somber note as a memorial service for Mrs. Abraham's husband. After the service, everyone moved outside to unveil the church sign and a dedicatory plaque for the church's courtyard.

A picture of Brother Abraham on the sign brought many in the crowd to tears. Stanley and Joshua stood by their mother as she wept. I walked closer to the courtyard sign and felt the hair stand up on the back of my neck as I encountered an unexpected surprise. Next to the picture of Brother Abraham was a picture of my mother, Delores, in honor of contributions she had raised by selling cookies so the church could dig for a water well. My mom and Brother Abraham had a special bond. As I gazed upon pictures of two very dear people now with the Lord for eternity, I couldn't keep the tears from falling on the Indian soil. The day was a service of hope and joy. Everyone felt we had honored Brother Abraham's life and calling.

The trip provided rich soil in which the friendship between my family and the Bhasme family grew. Our time in Bangalore and Hubli offered many in our group the opportunity to see God working through believers in a place halfway across the world. I felt sure God wanted me to remain a part of Brother Abraham's ministry, and I left India eager to return.

In the next twelve months, I returned to India twice. My son-in-law Jacob, his twin brother, Jason West, and I traveled to Bangalore in August 2006. Jacob and I taught the pastors. Jason interviewed and photographed college students for a school directory. Jason and I traveled to a nearby village to look at a possible site for a new church for the ministry, while Jacob remained behind at the pastor's conference.

Our arrival in the small village generated a crowd of people filled with curiosity over a rare visit from Americans, as they gathered around our vehicle. They followed our every step through the village. A translator told me that some in the crowd believed I was a professional wrestler from the United States, due to my six-foot-three, 290-pound frame. They were asking for autographs. Needless to say, we left the village without signing any autographs.

I enjoyed the time with Stanley and Joshua as we planned together how to best move the ministry forward. I encouraged Brother Abraham's sons to continue with their father's vision but also follow the Lord's leading in doing things they were passionate about for the ministry. When it came time to leave, I assured Stanley and Joshua that we would come back soon.

I arrived back in India the following March, along with a student minister from an Abilene church. This time, I planned to stay in India for two weeks. The trip's agenda was similar to my first trip to the country. We hoped to see as many churches and pastors as possible. With a two-man team, we didn't have the challenges associated with moving a large group around a foreign country and so we traveled more quickly.

I also planned to visit the United States Consulate in Chennai with the hope that Stanley and Joshua could secure their ten-year visas to travel to the United States.

In the days prior to our trip, I felt a knot on the inside of my leg. It grew significantly in the short time before I left. The appearance and feel of the knot concerned me, but I told no one because I didn't want the trip to India disrupted because of doctors' concerns about my health.

Carl Delozer, student pastor at South Side Baptist Church in Abilene, and I left for the long trans-Atlantic flight. Once I sat in my seat I realized how tired I felt. My business partner and I had put in long hours for the last few months. I tried to blame my fatigue on that, but in the back of my mind a hint of anxiety told me it was something more. Could I have the same disease as my mother? I forced myself not to think that. It was too troubling.

This being my fourth trip to India, I had learned the value of asking my travel agent to secure bulkhead seats for the long flight. I was more thankful than ever for that on this flight. Brother Carl and I arrived in India without incident and after a brief reunion in Bangalore with Mrs. Abraham and her family, Joshua, Stanley, and I left for the U.S. Consulate in Chennai – the site of severe damage when an earthquake in the Indian Ocean caused the Boxing Day Tsunami.

By the time we arrived in Chennai, I felt severely ill. My health worsened quickly from what I guessed was food poisoning. We reached the consulate near St. George's Cathedral and prayed before our meeting. Upon introducing ourselves to the receptionist, the visa official called for Stanley and Joshua. I started to walk with the two brothers when the official remarked, "Sir, I will visit with Stanley and Joshua alone. You wait here."

To say the least, I was confused when the official denied my access to the meeting. For the first time in all my trips to India, I wondered, *What am I doing here? I came all this way, I feel like death, and I failed to fulfill one of my major reasons for traveling eight thousand miles.* I sat under a stand of trees between the consulate and the cathedral, wanting to be home. I tried to muster the will to pray for Joshua and Stanley as I waited for them.

Finally, Stanley and Joshua emerged from the embassy. They had secured their ten-year visas and informed me I would be the sponsor for those visas. The news brought comfort to me. The ease with which the Bhasme brothers secured their visas was an answer to many prayers. Yet I still felt very sick, so we made a hasty return trip west to Bangalore.

I met up with Carl in Bangalore and regretted to inform him that my poor quality of health would require him to fulfill what remained on our objectives list. Under normal circumstances, I would have taken advantage of every second I had with Stanley, Joshua, and Mrs. Abraham to encourage them and love on their families. But my sickness worsened. I stayed in a hotel bed the rest of the trip praying for God's mercy and counting down the days to the return flight home. "Lord," I prayed, "I know You brought me here for a reason. Even if it was for me to learn you don't need me to accomplish Your work here, but You will always desire my willingness to serve. I trust You will equip Joshua and Stanley to care for the pastors, the children, and the college students. Lord, in this moment, I pray for a smooth flight home. I am grateful I have a friend to travel alongside me. God, I also ask that You comfort me and remove the anxious feelings I have about the knot in my leg. Father, I love You and thank You for the sacrifice of Your Son who has endured far greater suffering. Amen."

5

BLESSING AND CURSE

Carl and I landed safely in Abilene. With the stomach bug working me over while in India, I feared the eighteen hours of flying would push me to an even more intense level of discomfort. Fortunately, the Lord showed mercy and allowed a smooth flight home.

Once back in the United States, I struggled to regain my strength. The scale told me that I had lost twenty-five pounds in the almost two weeks I was away from home. A stomach bug in a foreign country is not a diet plan I recommend, and while I could stand to lose a few pounds, what I really needed was for my energy to return.

While in a foreign country, I can focus exclusively on ministry and connecting with new people. However, when I return home, the demands and to-do list become more diversified. I tried to balance the responsibilities of faith, family, and work, but found myself tiring unusually early in the day.

Before leaving for India, I had no problem starting work early and eating supper after dark. At first, I chalked up the limited energy levels to jet lag, fatigue, and my severe food poisoning, but I also became more concerned about the egg-sized knot in my leg. It had increased in size, so I had a friend with medical knowledge take a look at it. He was fairly certain it wasn't cancer, saying there might be a one-in-one-thousand chance of it being cancerous, but he also encouraged me to get a complete analysis done by my doctor. That's the only way to eliminate cancer and have complete peace of mind.

I scheduled a visit with my doctor. I approached the day of the appointment as I had previous challenges: I prayed, looked for what God wanted to teach me, and believed that the Lord would use the situation however it developed. After a consultation with my doctor, he referred me to a local surgeon to remove the knot for further testing.

I experienced a case of déjà vu. A little less than six years earlier, my mom went down a similar path. She had the knot on her neck. Next, her doctor wanted to remove the tumor. The mass ended up being cancer. I could see the same scenario play out in my life. In so many ways, I wanted to be like Mama in her ability to love people, but I certainly didn't want cancer to be something we had in common. However, if I did receive a cancer diagnosis, I would definitely do well to choose to receive the news like my mother did. Mama faced cancer with the same grace and strength she lived every day of her life. If she could handle my dad from the age of fourteen and could handle raising three children, then cancer was no match for Mama. Cancer ended her life prematurely, but it failed to take her faith and positive outlook on life.

In my own effort to remain optimistic, I made a list of the positives in my current situation. If, in fact, tests came back as cancer, as my mother's test did, I had a few things in my favor that could actually help me win the battle. First, I was considerably younger than Mama at the time of her diagnosis. Second, I had an edge physically over my mother. I worked out a couple times a week at the YMCA with friends. We mostly played racquetball, and a few of us occasionally lifted weights.

On May 9, 2007, I went through the procedure to have the

mass taken from my leg. Then I waited. We didn't expect results for another five days – five days of waiting for good news or bad news. I definitely wasn't thrilled at the idea of enduring the mental gymnastics of "what if." What if the tumor is cancer? What if the cancer is advanced? Not knowing the final diagnosis was worse than knowing bad news.

In this almost week of waiting, I became very introspective about my life as it related to God, to my family, and to my work. Two questions came to mind frequently related to God's pleasure with my life and whether my life fit the Lord's purpose. I surveyed my life as I had done before, during the loss of our child. Everyone at some point has a crisis of conscience. With the cancer diagnosis, mine lasted five days.

With the opportunity for reflection, I thought about my wife and children. Did Nancy know how much I cherished her? Did I spend too much time taking care of everyone else while neglecting my wife? I knew that my Heavenly Father had blessed me daily with Nancy's presence, and I took that relationship for granted. The diagnosis made me refocus on commitments I had made to Nancy.

Even though my daughters were out of the house, I wanted to make sure they heard from their dad more than just when there was a problem. Over the years, the girls and I made it a tradition to call each other at 11:11 a.m. to say, "I love you." I wanted to make sure I did that along with other gestures of love and affection. I wanted them to know how much they meant to me. I desired to hear their concerns when being a newlywed, nurse, or teacher proved overwhelming for them. Had I missed opportunities to do that while chasing my own dreams and managing my own challenges?

The following statement, recorded on May 14, 2007, presents a more complete picture of the personal struggle I felt to make things right:

*I have so many different feelings inside. First, is God
pleased with me? Next, am I the man He intended
for me to be? Does God want me to do something
different with my life? At this Y in the road of my
life, is this God's plan or a test of my faith? I have
testified most of my life about how God is in total
control in our lives. I have examined and reflected
with intensity for the past week. I have concluded
just how selfish and how sinful a man I have
become. I have missed my intended purpose in
several areas of my life. I have wasted opportunities
to share the gospel of Jesus Christ with people. The
Lord has given me so much, and I have wasted precious time.*

Out of this crisis of conscience, I became aware of my life in
a new way. I saw both the positives and the negatives of who
I had become. I clearly saw areas of growth or improvement
when previous bouts with pride had kept me from doing so.
I knew what I wanted out of life and trusted God to show me
how to get there.

On the day of this recording, five days after the procedure,
my doctor called. Nancy, Courtney, and Malory sat by me as
I took the call. I had tried in the days between the removal of
the tumor and the doctor's phone call to keep a smile on my
face and pray for good results. I answered my doctor's call and
heard the news I had dreaded but at the same time expected.
I had cancer. He was unsure as to the type of cancer, but I felt
sure it would turn out to be the same cancer as my mother. We
had to wait a couple more days to identify the type of cancer
and the course of treatment.

I wanted my family around me. I called Emily earlier that
afternoon and shared the news with her. We shed a few tears,

and Emily and Jacob made plans to come for dinner that night. Courtney and Malory were with me at the time of the call. They both stayed for the evening along with Phil. During the evening, we attempted to focus on the many blessings the Lord had given our family before this day and the blessings yet to come.

The day of my diagnosis and Courtney's due date were only a week apart. We anticipated the arrival of our first grandchild, Carson, and the great joy he would bring to our lives. We were able to praise God for His goodness and grace – that He gave our family this blessing to lift our spirits. Before the kids left for their homes for the evening, I asked Phil and Jacob to pray for me and for our family.

During their prayers, I thanked God for my family. I have a supportive wife who felt led to fast and pray for the next week. I was so glad that Courtney and Emily had married men who loved Jesus and wanted to lead their families to serve the Lord. I prayed that Malory would also find such a man. I cherished the way my three girls loved me and were concerned for me.

I recorded the following words on May 14, 2007, before going to bed:

> Well, the cancer path to the Y in the road has
> started. God is allowing me to start traveling down
> a new road. One I never would have chosen, but I
> will try to make the best of it. Here I go! I'm trusting
> my God!

I read in God's Word from Proverbs 3:5-6 that if I trust in the Lord with all my heart, the Lord promised to direct my path. The passage became my life verse. I have shared it with countless people living in the midst of affliction. The image of a path is important to me because the path should lead somewhere special according to God's plan. The path I imagined was a stone path – one in which the path constructor lays one stone ahead of the previous one until a road is constructed and the path is secure. In the early stages of my cancer diagnosis, I waited for the stones to build in front of each other one day at a time, trying to be patient as to where the path would lead.

The day after my diagnosis the word of my condition had gotten out. I received twenty-seven emails from all over the world. A great number of friends came by the house to pray and encourage Nancy and me. I talked with all my girls and sensed they were committed to trust God with me and to walk by faith. I knew they were worried, but I didn't want my diagnosis to take away their joy. I was especially concerned for Courtney and Carson. I trusted God to take care of Courtney and the baby in her womb in the final days of her pregnancy. I regretted that my cancer diagnosis coincided so closely with Carson's rapidly approaching birth day.

* * * *

At noon on May 16, I met Jerry Hallmark for lunch. Jerry is a great friend and the best business partner. We had worked together for over twenty-five years. The Lord used Jerry to keep me positive and to take my mind off cancer for the next hour or so. Our business was doing tremendously well, and we had plenty to discuss as we took time to retrace our history and develop a plan for how our work could go forward without me while I was out of town for a while. We had waded through similar discussions before, when Jerry faced health difficulties.

Jerry and I had started a multi-ventured business together after leaving the banking business. Our first venture was in the oil and gas business. Our specialty was reentering and completing old stripper wells, which are wells that produce small amounts of oil daily. This eventually led into drilling new wells.

The day we drilled our first well we felt incredible anticipation, believing we would strike it rich. Unfortunately, the well failed to materialize and we lost twenty-five thousand dollars. Nancy was extremely upset, and I was too. The loss was a horse pill to swallow, but we decided to continue forward. Jerry and I eventually raised enough capital through our stripper production to drill a second time.

At that time, and as the Lord would have it, Brother Abraham happened to be staying with us for a few weeks visiting churches that supported his ministry. Being a godly man and a dear friend, I asked him to join us in identifying the next place to drill and offer a prayer to bless our efforts. We were working hard, and my family needed to eat, so I figured the Lord wasn't against us. Brother Abraham encouraged me, saying, "Brother, I know you will succeed because you will help the people in India."

After my dear friend's prayer, nine out of the next eleven drilling attempts turned into tremendous producers of oil. While the Lord seemed interested in our children having food to eat and clothes to wear, the prayers didn't make the oil field work any easier or safer.

Working in the oil field proved the most demanding and dangerous work of my life. When we fought the rig and wells, we never knew when they might fight back. One evening I drove to a well site because a gas compressor was down. Before I restarted the compressor, I had to bleed gas off the line. It was a damp, heavy evening, and I made the mistake of not waiting to let the gas dissipate in the air. When I attempted to start the compressor, a spark ignited the gas, causing a minor explosion.

The force from the blast knocked me to the ground. The flame licked across my face and scorched my eyebrows, and burned the right side of my scalp and the hair on my arms. I made my way to the pickup and drove to Jerry's house as I neared the point of shock. After safely arriving at Jerry's by God's grace, he drove me to Abilene for treatment. Jerry and I eventually secured a buyer for our company, and we felt relieved to be out of the business.

We transitioned from the oil business to dirt contracting. We named our dirt business Lawn Tech and later added hydro-mulching and landscaping. Prior to this, Jerry and I built Wylie Swim Club, a private membership pool operating under family values and Christian standards. The pool was a great decision for our family, and each one of the girls took their turns managing the pool while in high school and college. Wylie Swim Club gave my daughters a source of income while teaching them how to manage employees and a business. They sold memberships, kept the pool clean, and ensured a family-friendly environment.

Our most recent venture was in the housing development business. Jerry and I developed Remington Estates and later Remington Storage. We bought the land years before for future development, but it sat for some time, giving Jerry a place to farm wheat. We eventually realized that the tap to Abilene water and sewer was just north of our land. This opened incredible possibilities for the land, and we contracted engineers to begin the development.

In business, some partnerships last and others collapse. My partnership with Jerry prospered, I believe, because we both sought to honor the Lord with our business and to use what God had bestowed upon us to help others in need. We worked as a team, treated each other fairly, and operated with the understanding that we wouldn't keep track of each other's hours on or off the job.

Jerry and I worked to take men in who were at a low place in life due to drugs, alcohol, or immaturity, and sought to build them up. By moving dirt, planting bushes, and raking out yards, men learned hard work, self-respect, and discipline.

We worked hard to provide for our families, but monetary gain was far from our most important mission.

* * * *

Jerry and I did more than reminisce over lunch at our meeting on May 16. We came up with a stable path forward for our company while things were less than concrete in regards to my health. After lunch, I met up with Nancy. Nancy and I went by the doctor's office to see if the results on the tumor had come in. The nurse looked up the information and said, "I'm sorry, we don't have your results yet."

Nancy and I were slightly disappointed in the delay and about to leave when the doctor opened the door to the waiting room and motioned us back in. As I walked into the consultation room, I steeled myself for his report. He motioned for us to sit in the chairs across from his desk. "We are certain you have non-Hodgkin's lymphoma." The news hit hard. He went on to say that further evaluation such as a positron emission tomography (PET) scan would clarify even further the state of my cancer.

I didn't hear much else he said. I wanted to call my mom's cancer doctor as soon as possible. We left the doctor's office and called to schedule an appointment with Dr. Olivares. Dr. Olivares agreed to see me the next day, so Nancy and I drove to Garland. We had a good rapport with Mama's doctor. I believed that if anyone could get the cancer into remission, he could. Several friends offered encouragement and reminded me that this type of cancer was very treatable.

On May 17, I walked into Texas Oncology for the first time as a cancer patient. I looked around the waiting room and read on the faces of others what I was feeling. It was an instant common bond with people I had never met before. Nancy and I saw people in the early stages of cancer like me, and we saw people who suffered from long battles with the disease. Evidence of chemo could be traced among the many bald heads and masked faces.

Some, try though they may, couldn't conceal the loss of hope. Sometimes you wondered who hurt the most: the patient or the caretaker. Others in the room demonstrated a confident spirit. In that oncology waiting room, an odd conglomeration of physical pain, weariness, uncertainty, and exasperation mixed with bravery, wisdom, and empathy.

Upon entering the consultation room, a significant uneasiness washed over me as I considered how I might fit into the cancer family. I wanted to be brave. I hoped to be an encouragement to those without hope. I also sought insight as to what the Lord might do through the process of treating my cancer.

Dr. Olivares remembered me from my mother's bout with non-Hodgkin's lymphoma. My precious mother had affected our shared doctor, and I have to say the visit with Dr. Olivares went as most first consultations do. We left his office with a plan. He ordered a PET scan and a bone marrow biopsy to see if the cancer was in my bones.

After the appointment with my new cancer doctor, we drove the short distance to my sister's house in Richardson. I needed to see my dad and sister. We enjoyed a meal together and more than anything, assured each other of God's plan in all of this while remaining realistic. For we all knew firsthand the stubborn nature of this type of cancer. We had seen in my mother how the cancer would go into remission but quickly come back. I wondered if that was the road I'd be taking on this journey.

The next morning we left Keith and Lorraine's house refreshed. Our overnight stay was only the start of the hospitality and love we would receive from my sister. Nancy and I drove the short distance from Lorraine's to Garland and my childhood home. I blamed it on a busy schedule, but I hadn't come back home as often as I would have liked after Mama's funeral. As I walked up the porch steps, I looked up to heaven and prayed, "God, will you let Mama know that I will be faithful and brave just like her?"

Dad opened the door. We sat down at the kitchen table together. He offered encouraging words and assured me everything would be fine. I knew he was still grieving over Mama's death and trying to be strong, but I could see he was struggling to get his mind around the fact that his oldest son had been hit with the same cancer that took his wife.

Nancy and I arrived home in Abilene prepared to rid ourselves of the worry connected to a cancer diagnosis. I had enough of the cancer business the last two weeks and wanted to think about better things, like a grandson to welcome into the world. On the night before Carson's arrival, Nancy and I went by Courtney's house to assure her the delivery would go well. Since it was her first baby, the anxiety and excitement blended into one emotion of "I can't wait to get this baby out!" I predicted Carson would weigh eight pounds and two ounces, and Courtney and Phil presented me with a cap that bore my new name: "Coach."

Carson gave us all a smile when we really needed one. He came into the world as a much-loved little boy. Nancy and I returned home from Hendricks Hospital on May 22, 2007, and I recorded the following reflections upon that day:

> *I will never forget this day. I met my first grandson,*
> *Carson Blake Cochran. He weighs eight pounds*
> *four ounces and is twenty inches long. He has blue*
> *eyes and strawberry-blond hair, and he looks just*
> *like his Coach. Coach is the name young men have*
> *called me who I have coached through the years and*
> *it will work for my grandchildren. Courtney did*

wonderful, and Phil did well. I give both an A+. Phil and Courtney will make great parents.

Everyone was there. Oh, what joy a baby can bring to the family. All of our thoughts for the day were on one baby and not on my battle with cancer.

I hope Emily and Jacob will be next. I saw the joy in their eyes, and they were so excited. I am also excited for Nana. She is the true unsung hero for our family. She is a wonderful wife, mother, mother-in-law, and now Nana.

Our prayer is that Carson will grow up to be a great man of God. I love you, Carson.

Carson's first day in the world brought my family together to celebrate God's greatest gift, the gift of life. The presence of a new grandchild gave me increased motivation to rid cancer from my life. I anticipated dove hunting, bass fishing, and teaching Carson how to run the backhoe. A couple of years later and Carson would be able to identify an excavator from a maintainer. I would like to think his fascination with heavy equipment comes from his Coach.

I worked less than normal during this time to prepare for my introduction to chemotherapy. I focused on exercise and improved nutrition to counteract the growth of cancer in my body. Nancy and I received phone calls, prayers, and visits that brought blessing upon blessing, but I knew my condition was worsening. The results from the PET scan proved to be far worse than what I thought. The cancer was all over my body and in stage four, which is the most advanced stage. I had a real battle on my hands.

In the evenings, when the calls stopped and the day calmed, I longed for the comforting presence of my mom, who would say with such peace, "I love you, Dale Richard." She had been my rock. I longed for the strong presence of Brother Abraham who provided encouragement to be a Godly father, husband, and businessman. He had been like iron. However, I would learn to rely on my wife, my children, and their husbands. People I had tried to be a rock and iron for would now stand in the gap to strengthen me.

The day before I left for chemotherapy I was at a low point physically. I had followed the doctor's orders and changed my diet and started taking a tray full of vitamins. All were defensive measures. In spite of the lifestyle change, tumors developed all over my body. I was fatigued and ready to roll with the treatment.

The pain associated with the knots increased significantly. I had large, red knots budding on the sides of my head. I spent most of the day in bed. My daughters, sons-in-law, and wife gathered around me in my bedroom. We prayed and sought to assure each other that God had a plan. I borrowed language from my football days and said, "For the last two weeks, we've been playing defense. Now it's time to play offense."

In June 2007, I started the CHOP program Dr. Olivares prescribed. CHOP is a common regimen for lymphoma patients with each letter standing for the drugs used. Nancy and I put many miles on our Yukon as we traveled between Dallas and Abilene. During the course of treatment, I learned so much more about lymphoma. I tried to relay to my friends and family what I felt they needed to know without unnecessarily alarming them.

On June 7, my family got together for a special lunch. In spite of my loss of taste due to the chemo, I had a tremendous appetite. A little extra pepper and salt gave my torched taste buds the pleasure of tasting something. Without extra seasoning, food was simply a solid to chew and not a flavor to enjoy. My kids liked to see me eat as well.

Over the course of the meal, the girls were curious about

how chemo was affecting me. We wondered when certain side effects might begin to appear. I shared what Dr. Olivares had told me in regards to the nature of non-Hodgkin's. The cancer is treatable but not curable. I could achieve remission, but I would one day have to face the cancer again. We would deal with that when and if it came.

For Father's Day, June 17, Nancy and I spent the day at the Malakoff farm with Malory, Courtney, Phil, and Carson. This was Phil's first Father's Day, and I could relate to the pride shining in his eyes as a new dad. Emily called to wish me a special day from Weslaco, in the Texas valley. She was serving along with Jacob on a mission trip with their church, but made sure to let me know how much she loved me and prayed for me. I never grew tired of hearing this from my daughters. Their love meant so much, but at the same time, I also wished I wasn't the source of concern.

After visiting with Emily, I asked Courtney if she wanted to go on a four-wheeler ride with me around the farm. We hopped on the two-seater and took off. I drove and Courtney sat behind me. As we cut through the pasture, the wind did more than breeze through my hair. It actually blew it off into Courtney's face. Upon returning to the lake house, I asked Nancy to shave my head on the front porch. Later, on a trip to New York City with friends, the hair of my goatee started falling out. We took many before-and-after photos of me with and without a goatee to document the chemo's affect upon my body.

Over the next few months, I kept up the regimen of chemo, blood tests, and a healthy diet. With every treatment, the tumors diminished in size significantly. This assured me that the plan was working.

In the fall, my family gathered for Thanksgiving. Thanksgiving is the largest meal Nancy prepares all year with all the usual menu trimmings. The turkey, sweet potato casserole, and chocolate pie are my favorites. Nancy and the girls worked for hours to make the meal special.

After lunch, we watched the Cowboys game, a Texas Thanksgiving tradition. This Thanksgiving had an extra measure of thankfulness. I felt we were all about to receive an early Christmas gift when I could say I was in remission. My doctor had me scheduled for a PET scan the next week, which would prove whether my gift of remission would find its way onto Santa's sleigh.

What transpired over the next few months was nothing short of God displaying His power. After Dr. Olivares's CHOP program, a change in eating, and constant prayer coverage, I received news that I was, in fact, in remission. We celebrated the news wholeheartedly and enjoyed a time of improved health. I stayed on my new eating plan and campaigned for others to join me. My life started to adjust to a new normal. Cancer had changed the way I saw life and the way I saw the world. I approached each day eager to make the most of my opportunity to be a healthy man for the Lord.

With the understanding that the cancer would more than likely return, Dr. Olivares decided to be proactive and have me take regular doses of Rotoxin. This drug served as a deterrent to the development of cancer in my body. The treatment held the cancer away for almost a year, but late in 2008, I felt the tumors growing once more. With Dr. Olivares already on top of my situation, we started a stronger chemo drug, and I soon went back into remission.

I stayed in remission for another year, but the cancer returned once more in 2010. After a couple of months of treatment, the PET scan showed no active cancer in my body. I had once again seen my cancer enter remission. Of course, my family and I were grateful for the news, but we also realized it was only a matter of time before the cancer returned.

What we never considered is that the cancer would remain in remission for a measly month. Returning to Dr. Olivares, he informed me that he had reached the limit of his service. He referred me to Dr. Robert Collins at the University of Texas Southwestern Medical Center (UTSW). On July 9, 2010, I had an appointment to determine the next step in my battle.

Under Dr. Collins' care, we decided to hold off on more chemo. My blood had really taken a beating from the collective rounds of chemo. The negative effects on my blood and organs required eleven Neupogen shots in one month to raise my blood counts. Dr. Collins' theory was that the chemo was doing more damage than the cancer. He would monitor the cancer and let my body recover as long as the tumors didn't impede my critical organs' ability to function.

My doctor also entered me into a trial study that would isolate cancer cells from a tumor removed from my body. Scientists would retrieve proteins from the cells, duplicate the genetic blueprint from the proteins, and introduce the proteins into the leaves of tobacco plants. The tobacco plants naturally reproduced these proteins. Scientists then harvested the proteins and made a vaccine from the proteins designed to boost my immune system with the antibodies to fight tumor cells in my lymph nodes. I didn't know if such efforts would amount to anything, but I agreed with the hope that it might help someone with non-Hodgkin's years down the road.

6

HOPE AND HELP

After reading the first five chapters of this book, you might conclude this is an overly sad story about suffering and hardship. I want to assure you that this story isn't a lamentation. My story is a journey of physical healing and spiritual healing – of recovery both my body and my faith.

In this life, we can't escape the pain of having our most precious relationships pried away from us. To lose my mom wasn't easy. To lose our child was a low point in our marriage. The loss of Brother Abraham brought with it an unexpected episode of sadness. Yet I am confident my mother, my mentor, and our infant child are with Jesus. This knowledge and belief brings comfort to our hurt and separation. I look to the Lord to see what He will teach me through loss and sorrow. The psalmist expressed a similar sentiment, saying, *Make me to understand the way of thy precepts: so shall I talk of thy wondrous works* (Psalm 119:27).

Due to the cancer diagnosis, I now faced a challenge within my own body that I hadn't faced previously. Knowing I had cancer wasn't even half the battle to come, as all people suffer, experience illness, and bury family members.

My story isn't really about recovering from cancer. In my life, the doctor on four occasions had told me the cancer was in remission. These words were a wonderful blessing. Remission gave me the chance to see more birthdays, more t-ball games, and more holidays. I wished everyone with cancer could experience remission after the treatment of cancer, but in some situations, the diagnosis comes too late in the cancer's advancement upon a person's critical organs. In these cases, treatment would be in vain. Other cancer patients grow too weak and can't continue treatments even if they make slight improvements.

Clearly, not all of us will experience healing and recovery as I have, but we can all experience the miracle of God that transforms a hurt in our lives into something good. Paul wrote in Romans: *And we know that all things work together for good to them that love God, to them who are called according to His purpose* (8:28). I have experienced Paul's teaching repeatedly. Notice that he says "all things" – that includes the good and the bad.

How easy it is to fall into the trap of loving God but missing opportunities to serve the Lord because illness, depression, selfishness, or anger creates a mental haze we struggle to see through. I believe God has a purpose for every situation. God doesn't love evil or intend for evil to take up permanent residence in one's life, but He can use anything for a purpose if we aren't so overwhelmed by the physical or spiritual challenge and fail to take hold of the opportunity. This requires trust in the Lord's strength. I have formed my convictions from the Bible and the wisdom from Proverbs 3:5-6: *Trust in the LORD with all thine heart; and lean not unto thine own understanding. In all thy ways acknowledge him, and he shall direct thy paths.*

The initial word in the proverb is *trust*. Trust is a non-negotiable with the Lord. In many facets related to our various business ventures, the ability to sign a deal requires negotiating. We are always willing to collaborate so everyone involved feels they have received a good deal. However, when it comes to our relationship with our Maker, some items are non-negotiable. This is true when it comes to trust.

Our natural inclination is to trust in the physical realm, including our health or physical capabilities. We convince ourselves that a healthy life is a purpose-filled and blessed life. We also place our trust and confidence in the dollars we earn, invest, and save. Our emergency funds, insurance, and retirement funds allow us to sleep easier at night. We assume the best path in life is a path of luxury. In walking this path, we find no reason to put a check on our drive to spend.

This is clearly not what the proverb teaches. God's people are to trust in the Lord and in His provision. We communicate this trust in the Lord through prayer. In meaningful prayer, we lay our hearts open before God but not to ensure God's protection of our wealth, bank account balances, or blood counts. A pastor once observed that in all of Paul's prayers, he rarely petitioned for a better emperor, for protection from marauding armies, or even for bread for his next meal. We vulnerably expose all of our existence, both seen and unseen, in prayer, in order to ensure travel on God's path.

After I had passed through the fog of shock over my non-Hodgkin's diagnosis, I prayed that God would show me why I had cancer. What purpose would this journey serve for my family, for my work, and for my faith? I prayed "without ceasing" but received no clear answer or direction. The lack of an answer created a temporary faith crisis that coincided with my physical crisis. Not only had the cells of my body failed me, but I also felt God delayed his response to my prayer unnecessarily. At this time in my bout with cancer, I entered a spiritual desert for several weeks.

While I struggled spiritually, the treatment showed promise with early success in attacking the cancerous tumors in my body. In fact, Dr. Olivares's course of treatment brought dramatic results. Along with that, I learned to trust my doctor. Plus, I learned that attitude is important and I tried to walk into the chemo room with a smile on my face.

Then there was the change to my diet. Prior to cancer you wouldn't have found a shred of green on my plate. I never enjoyed anything like salads or broccoli. Instead, my pre-cancer appetite called for a steady diet of BBQ and chicken fried steak. After cancer, salad became tolerable. When I saw a cookie or a glass of sweet tea, I reminded myself of something I read in Patrick Quillin's book, *Beating Cancer with Nutrition*. Sugar would only feed my cancer. So I didn't cave in to such temptations, but rather I attacked my cancer like a well-balanced offense in football. We hit it with chemotherapy, a new diet, and prayer. I wanted the cancer completely obliterated from my body.

All three of these "offensive moves" worked together to create a set of incredible before-and-after pictures. Before I started the cancer treatment, I had some hair, and I lost it. Before I started the cancer treatment, I had some weight to lose, and I lost it. However, the most incredible before-and-after photo wasn't an external photo but rather an inside picture of my body. The PET scan of my body before treatment was a ghastly sight. When I looked at the scan, the organs looked enlarged and distorted. Cloudy spots appeared all over my body. It was all cancer. The human body has hundreds of lymph nodes. Every lymph node in my body had cancer.

I knew through the course of treatment that the tumors diminished significantly in size, but the PET scan following my last chemotherapy treatment will forever be my favorite "after" photo. Not a smidge of cancer was visible in the scan. I had gone from stage-four non-Hodgkin's Lymphoma to being completely cancer free. The clear results from the scan were exactly what Nancy, my family, and I had prayed for God to provide. God brought about healing through prayer, treatment, and a changed lifestyle, and I saw the clear scan as answered prayer. The joy we all felt is hard to put into words.

However, before all of this, the Lord's first answer to prayer came during the course of treatment. God did something else through the course of treatment, which allowed me to grasp further Paul's teaching in Romans. I had experienced an improved physical condition. My body's betrayal of my will to live was subdued for the time being. Yet I still struggled to know the "purpose for this calling." Why did I have cancer? I knew the physical and medical reasons, but what I sought went deeper than biology. I felt my physical condition would somehow affect my spiritual condition and perhaps the spiritual condition of family, friends, and people I didn't know yet.

After my second round of chemotherapy, Nancy and I drove to Dallas to stay the night at my sister's house. Keith and Lorraine were always so generous to let us stay in their home. I learned not to protest when they offered their own bed and spacious bathroom downstairs, but to simply appreciate and receive their hospitality. Following a wonderful meal, I went to bed hoping for a good night's sleep before the chemo the following morning. The Lord had other plans.

I woke up abruptly around 2:00 a.m. and heard in my mind the following words: "Feed people physically and spiritually." The statement circled through my mind three or four times. To say I became excited is an understatement. God's silence toward my condition ended! In that moment, I left my own spiritual desert and entered a land flowing with milk and honey.

In the first few months of living with cancer, I discovered my life was in a fully unacceptable place in many realms. I wanted to be an active dad, a responsive husband, and successful in my partnership with Jerry. Cancer, left unchecked, would eventually rob me of all such opportunities.

I saw a similarity to the Hebrew people in Egypt. Moses,

Aaron, and the Hebrew slaves found the conditions of their lives intolerable and no longer acceptable. The only option for real human dignity was to leave the land and lifestyle for a place of freedom, peace, and rest. The process for leaving would take courage and trust. Placing his trust in God, Moses had a front-row seat to watch God change Pharaoh's heart, divide the Red Sea, and feed the desert wanderers with manna and quail.

In my own experience, I entered the process by agreeing to chemotherapy. Treating the cancer cells in my body with chemo created feelings similar to those experienced by the Old Testament wilderness wanderers. At times, the Hebrew people became irritated over food selection and lack of water, to the point they were ready to turn around and return to the unacceptable land of slavery. Acting out of fear, unpleasantness, and ignorance of God's presence can overcome the most positive attitude as treatment and its side effects linger on.

Eventually, the Lord moved beyond the sinfulness and insecurities of the Hebrew people and raised a new generation, led by Joshua, as they entered the Promised Land. Once in the Promised Land, it would be nearly impossible to return to the former life of enslavement and horrible working conditions.

In my case, chemo worked tremendously well in subduing the cancer to the point of remission. Remission is, for almost every cancer patient, like finding the Promised Land. The challenge with my situation is that the Promised Land of remission wasn't the ultimate place of peace and blessing. I had a different journey which completely took over the cancer journey as the ultimate priority.

I struggled to know the place and path God had for me during this most dreaded, unacceptable place in life. Once I understood my place and condition, I committed to a process of faithful prayer – to wait on the Lord. I approached this process as seriously as the cancer treatment regimen, and followed the spiritual plan laid out by Joshua when he said, *Sanctify yourselves: for tomorrow the LORD will do wonders among you.* The wonders Joshua spoke of reference God's protection as the Hebrew people finally walked across the bed of the Jordan River to the land of Canaan after a forty-year process.

Hearing from Dr. Olivares that I no longer had cancer was a banner day in my life. However, the joy and peace associated with that can't compare to the freedom and serenity I felt when the Lord concluded my journey from the spiritual desert land of uncertainty when I heard: "Feed people spiritually and physically."

I looked over at Nancy in bed next to me, eager to tell her about the opportunity God had blessed me with because of my condition. She was sleeping soundly. I tried to contain my excitement but couldn't wait to tell her what God had instructed me to do. "Nancy, Nancy." I woke her up. "Nancy, I know why I have cancer."

Her eyes fluttered open. She lifted her head from the pillow and muttered something like, "Great, can we talk about it in the morning?" She laid her head back on the pillow and instantly fell back to sleep.

Since I couldn't share with Nancy right then, I decided to call my pastor. No surprise to me now, but since I called at 2:00 a.m., he didn't answer his phone. I got up and walked out into the living room. Light streamed through the glass door in Keith's computer room. I spotted him sitting at the computer working, so I walked into the room.

My brother-in-law, Keith, a computer genius highly sought after in his field of expertise, was, more importantly, a fine father and leader in his church. He and my sister, Lorraine, had encouraged numerous young couples through their early years of marriage. Many of these married couples grew in their knowledge of the Bible by attending the Bible study class Keith taught for over a decade. Over the years, my brother-in-law and I had discussed the Bible extensively, along with practical matters of faith. This special relationship gave me the confidence to share how God had interrupted my sleep minutes before.

When I explained how God had answered my prayer in the middle of the night, he gave me simple advice: "Write everything down."

I did just that. I walked back into the living room, took a piece of paper, and wrote at the top of the page: "Feed people physically and spiritually." Over the next couple of hours, the Lord helped me see that I had cancer so I could be an encouragement to others battling cancer. The Lord brought to mind the pained faces of the people next to me in the chemotherapy room. My Heavenly Father also brought to mind the stories of suffering from men and women both young and old. Cancer was wrecking lives. The wreckage needed a compassionate, Christ-like response, and God called me to minister in His name to the hurting.

How could I do this? My idea wasn't over-the-top creative but rather very functional. I wanted to put together bags – tote bags – and to make them available to cancer patients. I hoped to fill them with resources related to their physical and spiritual condition. From experience, I knew that once a person learns they have cancer, a hunger for information arises like a sponge sucking up water. I planned to stock the bags with Christian music, a Bible, the book by Patrick Quillin, notepads, and pens. To start, I planned to take the bags with me when receiving treatment and to give them to the other patients, but I also wanted to make them available to anyone who knew of someone battling cancer. As the pieces started to fall into place in my mind, I also received a name for the ministry: Hope and Help.

In the middle of the night, God gave me a source of light for my own soul. He wanted me to be light in the dark world of cancer. People needed hope, and I had hope in Christ. People needed truth, and I had the source of ultimate truth in God's Word. People needed practical encouragement for day-to-day decisions related to their health and nutrition, and I had valuable information from Dr. Quillin.

I wasn't a nutritionist, but I had seen, in my own body, how tough decisions related to diet made a significant difference. The greatest source of personal light came in that God had answered my prayer. God had a plan and purpose for me even in my battle with cancer. My affliction with cancer wouldn't be in vain.

One thing my family knows about me is that once I have a task to do, I am highly motivated to accomplish that task. I am also not afraid to ask my immediate family to make it a priority as well. What can I say? My passion to accomplish this new ministry went beyond any entrepreneurial drive I had ever felt in business or banking.

Nancy and I started the ministry by buying Bibles at bookstores; plus we bought every book by Dr. Quillin we could find. Our pastor found blue bags to hold the supplies, and we gathered CD recordings of a message from an area pastor and CDs from our church's music ministry that featured hymns and songs of encouragement. To that, I added stacks of paper tablets and pens I had picked up at our local office supplies stores. Back at our home office, Nancy helped me organize the supplies and fill the bags.

I couldn't believe how doors opened for this ministry in the weeks to come. Upon returning to Dr. Olivares's office, I shared with him our vision for the ministry. I hadn't asked anyone to give or assist financially to this point, but I couldn't hide my pleasure when Dr. Olivares asked if he could help. He walked back into the room with a five-hundred-dollar check. It was the first official contribution to our ministry. Along with his financial assistance, he also offered to help distribute the bags through his office.

Then I had another idea. I decided to contact Dr. Quillin. Through a series of calls and conversations, he provided the books to our ministry at cost and didn't charge for shipping. His book had provided incredible wisdom and information for me, and I was incredibly grateful for his support for our newfound ministry. Dr. Quillin's embrace of our ministry was a tremendous boost to our efforts.

In the early weeks of Hope and Help, I had the opportunity to meet Bart Millard, lead singer for MercyMe, at a concert held at Beltway Park Church in Abilene. MercyMe had recently released the song *Bring the Rain*. The song became a theme song for me. If I heard the song on Christian radio, it encouraged me every time, because *Bring the Rain* was my life story.

When I sat down across from Bart I related to him my story and ministry, and he shared with me his own encounter with cancer. His father had died of cancer a few years earlier. He knew as an immediate family member the incredible struggle related to cancer and the spiritual encouragement needed to cope through the diagnosis, treatment, and potential death. Bart expressed great enthusiasm for my ministry and graciously responded to my request to make *Bring the Rain* available to our ministry. With his permission, we made a CD with his song and my testimony to place in the Hope and Help bags.

I placed a card in the bags for people to reach me if they wanted further information or knew of someone else who might need a Hope and Help Bag. My phone started ringing constantly with requests to provide bags. One call would be from a person who had cancer. The next call could be for a spouse. The next call possibly for the caller's child. Nancy and I tried to fulfill every request.

Then came requests to speak at cancer-related benefits and

fundraisers. I shared my story, my faith, and my purpose. Resources and funds started to pour in to the ministry. This support made it possible for us to expand the scope of our reach. The Lord opened a tremendous opportunity to feed people spiritually and physically, and we were able to do this for thousands of people.

As the ministry grew and the number of requests grew to more than two thousand, we could no longer fill the tote bags at our home. I went to the pastor of our church and asked if books and resources could be stored at the church. He agreed and suggested that those in attendance on Wednesday nights help fill the bags. At this point, the work of filling the tote bags transitioned from a two-person team to an entire church of volunteers. This took a tremendous burden off Nancy and freed us to focus on visiting with the recipients of the bags.

The way Hope and Help exploded made it very evident God's hand was directing. It had little to do with who I was before cancer. Before cancer, I perceived myself as physically strong and energetic. The people I visited and prayed with didn't care about my work ethic or business success. Cancer patients were much more interested in how I became weak and then how I became strong. Cancer patients have an incredible appetite for information. Hearing the story of a survivor brings incredible encouragement and hope. It didn't matter that my form of cancer didn't elicit the kind of fears that lung cancer or pancreatic cancer produces. Cancer is cancer, and I was willing to share my fight with cancer. I also wanted to share my fight with sin and victory in Christ.

Many conversations focused on diet. Often, I walked into a home to find everyone chowing down on pizza and cake. Equipped with my new knowledge, I said, "You can't eat this anymore." One problem was related to well-wishers. When people heard someone was sick they brought sweets, candies, and cakes. I taught people how to say thank you for these thoughtful gifts but to throw those foods in the trash because sugar feeds cancer.

However, what I encountered most was fear. In one sense, people feared how their families would cope. What would happen to their children if they died? What would happen to their spouse if they died? I understood this fear. People also communicated a fear of death itself. They wanted to know for sure what would happen after death. I am grateful that God used my cancer to open opportunities to share with hundreds of people how to surrender their lives to Jesus and walk with Christ.

That night at Keith and Lorraine's was the night God answered my prayer and revealed the purpose of my calling as the Lord created in me the idea for Hope and Help Ministry. Early that morning, I envisioned the people I would meet. I considered their stories and my response to their situations. God could use my story and my experience as an encouragement to others.

I never for one minute, anticipated that God would use my personal victory with cancer as an encouragement for a young child under the age of two, and worse yet, that this little baby would be my granddaughter.

7

BLESSED ASSURANCE

The tick of the clock grew louder by the second as Nancy and I, along with Courtney, Emily, and Malory, waited for Dr. Collins to enter the room. I silently checked the time on my phone – 1:30 p.m. The date was November 4, 2010.

My family rarely talks in a library-soft voice, but when you wait for life-altering news from the doctor, words distract from the mental what-if game. Something new and much more serious held my body and mind in check from being a patient husband, a playful grandfather, and a conscientious dirt contractor.

As we waited in the small white room with the customary examination table, handwashing station, and rolling chair, Jacob entertained my third grandchild, Ellie, in the commons. Ellie climbed over furniture, read books, and examined the monstrous, orange spiral art display inside the entrance to University of Texas Southwestern Medical Center in Dallas. My granddaughter exhibited a carefree spirit that could not be found among the rest of us.

Back in the small room, Dr. Collins' voice approached the door from the corridor. I had wondered for days what he would have to say. Would it be bad news or good news? The door opened. Dr. Collins greeted us as he sat formally upon

the small rolling chair. By his posture, I sensed he was ready
to get straight to the point.

* * * *

This latest chapter with my health had started two weeks prior
in Abilene. I had climbed into my dump truck ready to haul
a load to a job site. I prepared to drive down the hill from the
pinnacle of a gravel mine, and, like always, I approached my
vocation with energy. Work was something I had always seen
as a blessing from God.

Early in my childhood, my father taught me the blessing
of work. Daddy also demonstrated how to work diligently.
We planted multi-acre gardens, worked the farm orchards in
Malakoff, raised cattle, and often packed a week's worth of
work into one weekend. He also taught me the importance of
blessing the Lord with a portion of what I earned, as the Bible
instructs in Leviticus and Malachi. He said these were words
from the Lord.

My first opportunity for employment came when I was a
kid living in Garland. A lady on my street asked my dad if I
could mow her lawn. She paid me three dollars for my labor.
Three dollars! I can't tell you how excited I was as I clutched
the money in my hand and waited on the front-porch steps for
my father to return home from his job driving a delivery truck
for Safeway Grocers. As my father parked near the curb and
walked towards the porch, I waved the money proudly.

"Dale Richard," my father said. "Out of all the children on
this street God allowed you to be the boy to mow that lawn.
You need to tithe and give to God from what you earned."

"Daddy, what's a tithe?" I asked.

He answered patiently, "A tithe is ten percent."

"Okay. Daddy, how much is that?" I asked.

"Dale Richard, that's thirty cents."

My father taught me more than one important lesson on that entrepreneurial day. What work I receive is a blessing from God. The three-dollar job made me hunger for more work and more compensation. During high school, I wasn't much of a scholar, but I participated in sports, worshiped at our family's church, and worked until dark mowing and landscaping yards.

I can honestly say that my father's instruction remained with me through every job and opportunity, but I regret to admit that I didn't always follow his advice in regards to tithing. I knew I needed to tithe but didn't always feel I could afford it... On one occasion, Nancy and I clipped an IOU to God on the refrigerator door, but I don't recommend this practice.

I mention all of this because as I sat in the dump truck two weeks before, near the top of the gravel mine, part of my father's work DNA had made its way into mine. The work God had for me to do that day and in the days to come provided a new type of blessing – a blessing that alerted me to a significant development inside my body.

I put the truck into gear. Suddenly my left hand froze and gripped the steering wheel fiercely. In an instant, my hand wasn't responding to signals from my brain, or something of that nature. My hand wouldn't come loose and it wasn't steering the truck.

My mind raced. First, I had to stop the truck. Then – somehow – I had to release my cramped left hand from the steering wheel. With all the strength in my right hand and arm, I got the job done. With the truck safely stopped, and my hand off the wheel, I waited. Time ticked. My hand finally returned to normal after almost ten minutes.

In that window of time, I sat in the truck and mentally ran through the possibilities. Was this a stroke? Or was it something more? Did the flare-up have anything to do with recent events? Several times Nancy had said she noticed an unusual forgetfulness in me, and more than once I had failed to judge the distance between vehicles while driving. What was happening to me?

I took the unexpected break in my haul to call Nancy and alert her to what happened. For Nancy, these unexpected symptoms demanded the attention of my family practice doctor, Dr. Carl Trusler. I agreed but felt I could make it through the rest of the day. "Call the doctor for me," I said. And in typical stubborn fashion, I kept on working.

The next day I knew I needed to get to the doctor, but Jerry and I had important infrastructure work to do at a new housing subdivision he and I were in the process of developing. With every street, we dug sewer lines and manholes. In the midst of this work, I came across an unfinished manhole. The bottom of the hole looked uneven. I grabbed a pick and rake and jumped the three or four feet to the bottom.

The only problem was my rare inability to judge distances correctly. The hole was nine feet deep instead of three. I slammed into the side of the manhole wall with my forehead and narrowly avoided the pick puncturing my body's core. I was extremely rattled and dazed, feeling like I might pass out at any minute.

Paige, Jerry's stepson, had worked on the crew for a couple of years and had become quite skilled in operating every piece of equipment in our inventory. I also had the privilege of baptizing him at Broadview Baptist Church in Abilene.

When I jumped into the hole, Paige had been working on the lines with me. He saw me disappear into the manhole and quickly maneuvered the backhoe over to the manhole and pulled me out with the backhoe's bucket. After a half-hour of shaking the cobwebs from my head, I decided I'd done enough work for the day. I'd be better off resting at home. I drove the mile to our home and promised Nancy I would go see Dr. Trusler the next day.

Sitting in the doctor's office the following morning, I recounted the nerve-racking and painful events of the previous two days. I also shared some of Nancy's concerns in regards to my changing personality and recent struggle to recall names and dates. He wanted to check for a potential concussion and any other possibilities. Dr. Trusler scheduled me for a CT scan. After all the medical scans I'd endured, I handled it like a soldier and waited for the results at home.

I happened to be walking through my prize-winning peach tree orchard when my phone rang. It was Dr. Trusler. "Dale, is there a place where you can sit down for a minute?" Unfortunately, I knew a doctor never sits you down for good news.

I sat down on a bench in the midst of the trees facing a large stone cross. "I'm ready."

"Dale, I am sorry to tell you that the scan shows a large mass on the side of your brain. It could be cancer or a tumor."

Emotion formed a thickness in my throat. I struggled to breathe, to find my voice. I cleared my throat and said, "I'll contact Dr. Collins." After hanging up with my family practice doctor, I took the next few minutes to have one of the most frank monologues with God in my life as I stared at the cross. It went something like this:

> Lord, is this the way you want me to die? I am in
> remission for the third time in my life. I have reor-
> ganized my priorities. Nancy and I have a ministry
> to cancer patients. I am enjoying being Coach to my
> grandkids. This can't end this way right now.

In my state of confusion and disbelief, the cross in front of me triggered a swift transition in my mental mood. God used the stone cross as a tool to jog my memory... the last days of Jesus' life ended in horrific physical suffering. God knew what it meant for His own Son to suffer. I asked God to help me understand what the last days of suffering could be like.

After my time for prayer and reflection, I made a few phone calls. The first was to my father. The dread of more doctor offices, more needles, and more treatment made me long for an encouraging word from my mother. Five years had passed since her funeral. An "I love you, Dale Richard" from my mother would have given me a sense of peace, more than any word from any other person. Thoughts of Mom turned to thoughts of my father. How would he take the news? How would he respond to one more urgent call due to cancer? As the phone rang, I ran through possible ways for how to start the conversation.

"Hello, son," my dad answered with unexpected enthusiasm. My dad, in his mid-seventies, enjoyed the caller identification feature on his phone.

I tried to counter his enthusiasm. "Hi, Dad."

My father replied, "It's good to hear from you. What's going on for you today?"

Dread came over me. I hated to call under the circumstances, knowing that he would become concerned and lose the cheerfulness in his voice. I tried to answer with strength. "Well, Daddy, I had a few tests recently and a scan shows that I have a mass in my brain. It's probably cancer. I have to come to Dallas for Dr. Collins to evaluate."

Before I mention the significance of what my father said in response to my news, it's important for you to understand him better. To be concise, he is a pessimist to the core. For an idea of how his mind tracks, here are a few examples: if the family planned a trip, he'd warn about a probable flat tire. If you wanted to work in the yard, it would probably rain. If you drove the tractor, it would most likely break down. Dad always saw the glass as half empty.

However, on this day, my dad said something that bordered on the miraculous. He spoke to me with the encouragement of my mother. I can't remember his words exactly but his change in tone made a lasting impression. With all the upheaval in my life, my father had become an overnight optimist, and it happened at the best possible moment.

The second call went to Dr. Collins. I let him know about the scan and the two episodes that alerted me to go to the doctor in the first place. It was no surprise that he wanted me to come to Dallas as soon as we could pack and get loaded.

The conversation I had with my dad gave me the much-needed strength to call Nancy, Phil, and Jacob to relay the information to my daughters. I called Malory. The level of difficulty rose with each call. I wanted everyone to hug my wife and hold my daughters before I left for Dallas for answers.

When I awoke the next day, I hoped it had all been a bad dream. Unfortunately, the prior day was real life, with real phone calls, and real results to scans. On the real day after, Dr. Collins ordered an additional scan to guarantee the accuracy of the scan from Dr. Trusler's order. The results came back the same as before. Upon verification of the mass, Dr. Collins admitted me to Zale Lipshy University Hospital for a brain biopsy. Over the next twenty-four hours, I waited for the biopsy procedure as my doctor ordered more tests.

At this point in my life, I had persevered through more medically than I ever thought a person could endure. I had chemotherapy, CHOP programs, spinal taps, and a chest port inserted under my left collarbone, plus various surgeries. But this was new … it was more. Never before had I felt the screws of a biopsy halo turned into the side of my head. Nancy and my three girls stood by during the whole process. I wanted to be a strong Daddy for my daughters. I entered tough-man mode.

The technician spoke up. "Mr. Morrison, let me know when

this begins to hurt." Not two or three cranks into his work, I cried uncle. Tough-man mode quickly left me.

"All right. That's enough," I said with the hope that's all it would take to secure the halo. Unfortunately, the two twists were only the beginning. The technician took out a needle and started deadening the skin around the bolts. We waited a few minutes, and then, for the next fifteen minutes, he turned the bolts to secure the halo to my head.

Drops of perspiration, mingled with blood, trickled down my face as the surgery team rolled me to the operating room. The doctor performing the surgery knew my medical history and offered his sympathy for my situation. Suddenly, a wave of confidence came over me. I felt assured in the Lord's plan for my life. I said, "Keep up with me because I am going to live."

Our conversation turned to the procedure. For some odd reason, I asked the surgeon how he would access my brain for the biopsy. He picked up a drill in one hand and a probe with the other. Fortunately, the anesthesia started to do its work. The surgeon palming the drill was the last thing I remembered.

After the procedure, Dr. Collins sent the five brain samples to a research hospital in Bethesda, Maryland, for analysis. Nancy and I waited during the next week at home for the results. My family and I noticed a further decline in my mobility. I struggled mostly with the left side of my body. I strained to raise my arm, and I lacked the muscle control in my fingers to button my shirts, tie shoelaces, or cut up my food. Feelings of helplessness began to sabotage my resolve as my body weakened.

The evening before our consultation, Nancy and I drove to Dallas to stay with Keith and Lorraine. We planned to have lunch with our friends from Haiti, Jacques and Marie, before arriving at UTSW. I hadn't seen our dear Haitian friends since visiting them after the earthquake the previous February.

Jacques and Marie lifted our spirits tremendously. Right at

our table, Jacques and Marie prayed passionately for the Lord's healing for my body. We finished our time together and promised to let them know the results. Before parting ways, I shared with Jacque the same sentiment Brother Abraham shared with me before boarding his flight: "Brother, if I don't see you again, I'll see you in Heaven."

Now, Dr. Collins sat on the short rolling chair. He made eye contact with me and said, "Dale, you don't have cancer."

A felt a tremendous burden taken from me but Dr. Collins didn't smile; his look remained hard and serious. "That's a good thing, isn't it?" I asked.

He shook his head. "Not this time. We can only wish it was cancer. We can treat cancer. What you have going on in your brain right now is difficult to treat and incurable. You have a brain virus known as the JC Virus. Dale, the bad thing about this virus is that we can slow down the symptoms caused by PML, Progressive Multifocal Leukoencephalopathy, but unfortunately, we can't stop the growth of this virus. Over the course of the next few months, you will notice a similar lack of mobility on your right side as well. A few other issues will develop. You will eventually become blind. You will lose your ability to hear or talk. Your body will curl up into the fetal position, and you will die a slow death. That's it. You die. I want to assure you that we will do the best we can to keep you comfortable, but this is a horrible brain virus."

My doctor continued for a few moments but I wasn't fully listening. I wondered how the news was affecting Nancy and my daughters who were right behind me. Once again, my wife and daughters were enduring bad news about my health. My eyes remained focused on Dr. Collins as I processed the ominous news. In that moment, a sinking feeling inside me erased all confidence about healing. A question circled through my mind – a question I had considered only briefly before when diagnosed with cancer: *how long will I live?* I never recommend asking the question because the timing of our death is in God's hands, but it's what came out of my mouth.

Dr. Collins said, "I think you will enjoy Thanksgiving. Christmas will be a hard time, and you probably won't live long in the New Year. Dale, I'm so sorry. I have a virus doctor here that will be able to explain the virus better to you. Her name is Dr. Li."

I robotically nodded, but I really didn't know how much I could take. The news about PML-JC and its future impact on my body and livelihood was enough to absorb. As Dr. Collins readied to step out, Jacob and Ellie came into the room. It didn't take Jacob long to realize the news wasn't good. He looked into Emily's eyes red with tears and some of the color drained from his face. I introduced Dr. Collins to Jacob and said to my son-in-law, "We have a fight on our hands."

Dr. Li came into the room to fill us in on more issues related to the virus and the medicines taken to help with the side effects as the virus overtook my brain. Part of her explanation touched on how a person contracts PML-JC. She explained: "The virus you have is a waterborne virus that grows in people who have weakened immune systems like yourself. Somewhere you drank water not thoroughly treated for bacteria and viruses." I wondered for a moment where this might have happened in the last few months. Then I remembered the moment Ben Gray and I drank water cleaned by the filtration system in Haiti the previous January. Was it at that moment I became exposed? It would be a futile waste of strength to ever know for sure, but it was my best guess.

Dr. Li shared stories of various patients, along with the story of how cancer had affected her daughter's life. In the middle of our discussion, Dr. Collins appeared at the door and asked Dr. Li to meet with him in the hallway. Dr. Li stepped out and shut the door. They left us to wonder about the nature of their discussion. I tried to pick up a word here and there to guess what they needed to confer on rather abruptly.

The two doctors stepped back into the room and tossed my family and me a lifeline just in time, because, truthfully, we were going under quickly. Dr. Collins took the lead. "Dale, I think we might have a plan for an experimental treatment." We all perked up. Even though it would be experimental in nature, it gave us hope that the treatment might work.

Dr. Collins explained. "I had lunch today with a couple of doctors, and over the course of lunch we discussed the patients we had that afternoon. I shared about you and the bad news I had to deliver to a friend. I told the doctors you were a fifty-two-year-old male with a history of non-Hodgkin's lymphoma now diagnosed with the virus. One of the doctors said that his brother was in the midst of a trial study treating HIV patients who contract the same virus you have with a drug known as Interleukin-2. I think we should try the same thing with you."

I sensed Dr. Collins' optimism. Inwardly, I also thanked God for His perfect timing. While Jacques and Marie prayed for a path to healing at lunch, Dr. Collins was at lunch with a couple of doctors discussing their work for the day. The lunch put him at the right place at the right time to hear about a treatment he hadn't previously thought about for a cancer patient with the rare virus. I found the correlation between the two lunches very compelling evidence that the Lord's hand was involved.

This also meant I had a new doctor ready to attempt treatment of my virus. Not long after my meeting with Dr. Collins, I had an appointment with Dr. Benjamin Greenberg. He seemed excited to meet me and hear about my case. I was also glad to meet him, even though the treatment made me a science project. I expressed my hope that if it didn't save my life, then maybe it might help someone else later on. This was something

I learned from my mother's example. She always wanted to live long enough and experiment with treatment so that it could save someone else's life.

Dr. Greenberg used our time to share what he knew about Interleukin-2. "IL-2 is a treatment traditionally designed to boost the body's immune system to fight cancer." His study looked at how IL-2 could be used to fight a virus which develops due to a compromised immune system. By agreeing to the treatment, I was the first Non-Hodgkin's Lymphoma patient with PML-JC virus to receive IL-2. Dr. Greenberg hoped that treatment with this form of immunotherapy could give me more time to live, but he never used the word cure.

We stayed in Dallas not knowing when we would return to Abilene, but glad to know we had an option on the table. The experimental treatment kept us from coming home empty-handed, but even with this thread of hope, I knew what my body told me. The stroke-like conditions on the left side of my body worsened by the day. They kept me grounded but also tremendously burdened.

If I was to die soon, I had friends with whom I wanted to share the good news of eternal salvation. The Lord laid on my mind and heart close to twenty people. I wrote letters to the men I played racquetball with for the last eight to ten years. To some I wrote letters offering an invitation to meet with me to share the faith I had in Christ. Others I saw in person. Most were receptive. Very few declined. I enjoyed the conversations, and it turned out that these men were some of the first to notice the change brought on by the virus's growth. These men prayed for me each week, and I am so grateful for all they did on my behalf.

The lengthiest and most personal letter I wrote was to my friend and fishing guide, Danny Tamayo in Port Isabel, Texas. Jacob and Emily were traveling to McAllen, Texas, soon for a denominational meeting and planned to take one morning to fish with Danny. They delivered his letter personally.

If I was to die soon, I wanted Nancy to be secure. I didn't want the burden of the business put upon her. Jerry graciously agreed to buy my half of Lawn Tech. He also named our newest housing project Coach's Corner, in honor of my grandchildren calling me Coach. I sincerely appreciated the gesture.

I also wanted my daughters to be secure. Courtney and Emily had both married godly men and had started their families, while Malory was dating Steve Foster. They seemed to be a great match. Malory had completed her nursing degree, while Steve worked for an engineering company in Lubbock.

Steve joined the family during our brief return home before I started treatment. I felt he probably had intentions to ask Malory to marry him, but I wanted to make sure he understood the uncertain nature of my health and my desire to walk Malory down the aisle. I asked Steve to join me on a trip to purchase corn for the deer feeder.

While driving to the store, the moment I had looked for presented itself to ask Steve about his intentions. I glanced at Steve in the passenger seat and said, "I really want to be able to walk Malory down the aisle on her wedding day. So, if you plan to marry her, let's start planning for that day." Judging from Steve's steady response, he had already given the matter extensive thought. I appreciated his openness and most importantly his love for my youngest daughter.

In light of my condition, I also planned my funeral. I know some really struggle with doing this, but I wanted tough decisions made so Nancy wasn't left alone to make these plans by herself. I took all of these issues on with a sense of urgency, not knowing when I might go blind or be unable to speak.

Before treatment could begin, I underwent a series of tests that spanned from eyesight exams to walking prescribed distances. The tests allowed my doctors to see the full scope of my growing list of disabilities. During the vision test, the patient nurse had to prop my head up to complete the exam. With the passing of each day, I encountered new limitations. As a man that used my hands, arms, and legs to work hard to provide for my family, I felt robbed of the most valuable tools I possessed.

I arrived at UTSW on November 8 for the first treatment, knowing my closest friends and family were petitioning the Lord on my behalf. My friends in India, Ukraine, and Central America were praying for me too. Dr. Greenberg decided to start with 500 cc of IL-2. After each treatment, the protocol included an evaluation from both Dr. Greenberg and Dr. Collins of my body's response to treatment. On day two, I received the same dosage. On day three, Dr. Greenberg decided to double the dosage.

I woke up on day four of my IL-2 therapy feeling different. Again, Keith and Lorraine invited Nancy and me to stay with them for the duration of my experimental treatment. I stepped into their shower and to my surprise felt the warmth of the water on my left side. Over the last few weeks, with the deadening nerves in my body, I'd been unable to sense temperature. Then I raised my left arm! In that moment, in the shower, the bathroom became a private sanctuary for worship. I'm not talking about your normal singing-in-the-shower performance. I sang to God the lyrics from the great hymn *Blessed Assurance*. I carried the joyful worship in my heart as I finished preparing for the day.

Instead of telling Nancy the good news, I decided to show her. I called her over, and she walked towards me ready to tie my shoes as she had been doing for weeks. To her surprise, I grabbed my tennis shoe, placed it on my foot, and successfully tied the laces without assistance, though I only loosely tied the shoelaces. We praised God together.

I walked downstairs slowly, still depending on Nancy's

assistance to negotiate the steps. We made it into the kitchen to sit down for breakfast. My nephew, Caleb, stood next to a dish filled with oranges.

I looked at my teenage nephew and said, "Caleb, toss me an orange."

Caleb looked at me with a hint of doubt. He knew my limitations. "Are you sure about this, Uncle Dale Richard?"

I nodded and prepared for the toss.

He picked out an orange from the bowl and tossed it in my direction. I raised my left arm and caught the orange. His eyes grew wide with surprise, and I asked for a second throw. He shared in our joy as I caught the second orange. I asked for a third toss, but on the third attempt, my arm and hand weren't strong enough to catch the orange. Disappointment diluted my excitement enough that Caleb noticed.

"Don't worry, Uncle Dale Richard," he said. "We had a better completion percentage than the Cowboys did this past Sunday." Of course Caleb would say such a thing. The Brock family is mostly New England Patriot fans.

Caleb and Nancy's encouragement boosted my mood as Nancy and I left for UTSW ready to share the news. Upon arriving at Dr. Collins' office, I announced the good news to the nurses and doctor. To say Dr. Collins was enthusiastic about my improved mobility is an understatement. The medical professionals were in disbelief and shock. My friends and family celebrated the development.

A tragedy in the family cut short our celebration that day, however. Nancy's mother, Sarah Stevens, confined to a wheelchair for the better part of a decade, had fallen from her chair and suffered a severe injury. Phil, Courtney's husband, kept Nancy and me informed about Sarah's status. The medical staff was doing all they could to comfort Nancy's mother, but it was serious enough that they were unsure how long she might live.

We let my doctors know my schedule had to be changed. At first, they argued against us going to Abilene, but eventually gave up their fight. Nancy and I made what felt like the thousandth trip on Interstate 20 to be at Sarah's side when she went to be with the Lord. But on this trip, Nancy Capra, Jay Capra's wife, graciously offered to drive us from Dallas to Abilene, and back to Dallas. Sarah's passing was a reminder that at any time, our human happiness can turn to sorrow and that at such times the Lord will provide abundantly in our grief. One minute, Nancy and I rejoiced over catching an orange and tying shoe-laces, and in the next hour, we faced completely unexpected decisions and emotions. If we had learned anything in the past few years, we knew the Lord would never cease in His care and love for my family.

For the next two years, I continued daily injections of IL-2 into my abdomen. With periodic scans, the virus showed drastic reductions. In comparison to lab results taken November 8, the next report revealed the viral count in my spinal fluid decreased by 50 percent and my immune system improved by 20 percent. After giving the results, Dr. Greenberg said, "We're not out of the woods yet, but we're definitely going in the right direction."

At this point in the treatment process, I felt God had given me more time. I optimistically thought that maybe I would live after all. However, we still had a healthy measure of caution and realism regarding how difficult it would be to achieve ulti-mate healing. Nancy and I remained in the metroplex, living in the upstairs bedroom at Keith and Lorraine's Richardson home, thankful for their kind hospitality, but we missed our girls and grandkids.

I knew my girls had grieved over my situation, which added a heavy load upon their already demanding lives. I wanted to do something that would give us some quality father/daughter time. An idea finally came to mind. I invited Courtney, Emily, and Malory to Dallas for a little retail therapy. The girls eagerly agreed, and we set a day for them to come up.

On November 17, I went through my normal routine of driving to Dr. Greenberg's office, receiving the shot, and evaluating my progress. Nancy and I then met the girls at the Firewheel Mall near Lorraine's house. We had a couple of rules for the day. First, we wanted to keep the day upbeat. We had all cried enough. The girls agreed to limit the waterworks. Second, we would have fun. Check again. My daughters were onboard. Finally, I couldn't say no. I gave them carte blanche to buy whatever they wanted. From the looks on their faces, I had found the password to their hearts. They were ready to shop, and I was ready to see my daughters laugh and enjoy one another's company.

As we went from shop to shop, the stores' employees noticed something different about us. They asked if we were celebrating a birthday or a special occasion. I tried to give an explanation they could understand. The gift I received by having the day with my girls is worth so much more than the gifts Nancy and I gave that day. Even with so much uncertainty in our lives, we knew the bond within our family would remain strong.

* * * *

In February 2011, we celebrated a miracle. The scan showed the PML-JC virus to be completely dormant. Only scar tissue from the virus remained. Tests also detected no sign of the virus in my blood. With each day, I grew more confident about the nature of my healing.

If you had asked one hundred of my friends the previous November if I would live or die, ninety-nine would have said Dale is probably going to die. Jay Capra's father Dr. Donald Capra, an incredibly brilliant doctor who specializes in cancer research and whose medical knowledge I respect immensely, said, "Dale, I know you have shown some improvement, but there's no way you will defeat this."

I had become a tragic case, but clearly, the Lord had me follow Him on a different path. Dr. Greenberg later wrote to me and said that I had overcome a health nightmare with an 80-percent mortality rate; for most patients there would be no way to reverse the circumstances. Due to the efforts of Dr. Greenberg, Dr. Collins, incredible medical treatment, and the glory of God, we beat the odds.

Nancy, my daughters, and family entered into a season of celebration over my improved health and my daughter's upcoming wedding. Steve apparently understood my less than subtle prodding and proposed to Malory the first week in December. Not that he needed any nudging. I have beautiful, intelligent, and faithful daughters.

Over the course of time that Dr. Collins monitored my condition, I shared that if I lived long enough to see Malory get married in the spring, I wanted him to come down to witness the occasion.

"I wouldn't miss it," he said, but I really don't think he thought he would have the opportunity to fulfill that promise. Yet, on March 5, 2011, we gathered at Logsdon Chapel on the campus of Hardin-Simmons University for Steve and Malory's marriage ceremony.

Prior to the ceremony, I brought Dr. Collins into the reception room where Nancy and I waited along with the bridesmaids and Malory for the wedding to begin. With a day full of hugs and tears of joy, perhaps the most heartfelt embrace was the one I witnessed between Malory and Dr. Collins as she thanked him for his role in saving my life. Like the words found in the hymn of our faith, *Blessed Assurance,* the joy evident among us was a "foretaste of glory divine."

8

CALLIE'S BATTLE

Phil and Courtney sat across from Dr. Honeycutt in Cook Children's Hospital in Fort Worth. The three met in a consultation room to face the truth about their almost-two-year-old Callie's health and future. Nancy and I remained in the hospital room with Callie, our first granddaughter, and prayed for the meeting.

Dr. Honeycutt delivered an unimaginably dreadful report. Phil started to call family asking them to come to the room. With every call, the tone of Phil's voice and the cries of my daughter said it all. Amanda Toogood, one of Courtney's best friends, Jacob, Emily, Malory, Phil's parents, and Nancy and I crowded into the room.

The room transformed from a doctor consultation room to a place of serious pleading with God. I heard Emily praying as we entered the room. I witnessed our middle daughter crying out to God for her niece and Courtney's hurt and fear.

Emily prayed boldly: "God, we believe you will watch over Callie. You will strengthen us. God, please be with Callie and heal her. We want her to have a long life. We love her so much. God, we pray for Phil and Courtney. I know they are so afraid. We are all so afraid. We need You more than ever before. Help us to trust You. Lord, we pray for Callie's surgery tomorrow, that You will watch over the surgeon and that You will watch over Callie during the surgery. Lord, we are here for Courtney and Phil. Allow us to be an encouragement to them. I am so thankful that You gave Callie loving parents who love You and trust You. Lord, we believe in Your power, in Your strength, and in Your ability to perform a miracle. We trust You completely. Amen."

* * * *

The 2011 Memorial Day weekend found Nancy, my girls, sons-in-law, grandchildren, and me at South Padre Island. Callie, my twenty-two-month-old granddaughter at the time, looked toward the Gulf of Mexico water made murky by the sand rolling in the surf. Her smile surrendered to a nervous frown. She had happily played in the sand that my children had formed into castles years ago, but now the time had come for Callie to hop on the boogie board and take on some toddler-sized waves.

I, along with Callie's dad, Phil, held the board in shallow one-foot waves and let the children ride waves the perfect size for small children to enjoy. Carson, Callie's brother, rode the waves first; then her cousin Ellie enjoyed the fun, but Callie demonstrated less eagerness. Finally, her turn came, and she negotiated the board by rising to all fours. Phil and I held the board with one hand and with our other hand made sure Callie didn't fall into the water. The water, barely a foot deep, provided no real danger, but we knew that if she fell off the board we might have to wait until next year before Callie agreed to ride again.

For the first few seconds Callie held on with stiff muscles and maintained the same nervous look. However, little by little, the frown turned to a grin, until finally a big smile broke across her face, the waves being a source for her joy. We all celebrated her accomplishment.

The Morrison family trip to South Padre is a long-held tradition starting with my parents. For my high school senior trip, we camped on South Padre Island in tents. We swam in the gulf and waded into the water to fish.

During our time there, my mom became a source for quite the comical tale. My family and I stood near the waves casting our lines as far as we could launch them into the gulf's wind. Mama stood on the shore and cast her line. After every cast, her line would quickly wash onto the beach. Growing frustrated she exclaimed, "I want to go fish on the other side." In between laughter, we attempted to explain the impossible nature of her request to fish off the coast of Yucatan Peninsula.

Nancy and I came to South Padre on our honeymoon. Once the Lord blessed us with children, it didn't feel like summer for Courtney, Emily, and Malory if it didn't include a trip to the beach. As our daughters grew, the yearly tradition became something we all looked forward to. Some summers we invited other friends and extended family. After our daughters graduated from high school and went to Hardin-Simmons University in Abilene, they found husbands. Nancy and I invited them all – after all, someone had to carry the luggage.

Even though the size of the group changed, the nature of our activity really did not. French toast in the morning, hanging out at the beach, building sand castles, and taking long naps during the heat of the day filled our days while in South Padre. At night, we would find a restaurant to enjoy, our favorite being the outdoor dining at Louie's Backyard. The passing boats, the bay, the view towards Port Isabel, and after-dinner fireworks added aesthetic pleasure to the piles of crab legs and boiled shrimp.

Through the many years vacationing at South Padre, I made sure to find time for fishing. I really didn't care for deep-sea fishing out in the Gulf of Mexico, because when I was a teen in high school I found it to be an expensive way to become green with nausea.

Instead, I wanted to find a fisherman who fished the calm bay channels. After trying a few captains, an already booked captain introduced me to Danny Tamayo, known locally as the Barefoot Fisherman. (He got his name because he worked his boat without shoes.)

He brought his boat into a cove, grabbed his bait net, and jumped into the water to cast for fresh croaker. Danny only fished with fresh bait and it paid off. I limited out on trout. To put it truthfully, I couldn't have asked for a better captain. Danny had fished Port Isabel Bay since his childhood. His history with this swath of coastal waters meant he knew exactly how to fish the channels even with their rapidly changing depths and tides. Bottom line: Danny knew how to put you on the fish. If the fish weren't biting, he kept moving the boat from honey hole to honey hole until he found them. In the twenty-plus years of fishing at South Padre, Danny is the only captain to take my family out on the north and south channels of Port Isabel Bay. He even humbled himself a few times by guiding for dolphin-watching trips.

When our daughters had children of their own, the number of people on our trips grew rapidly, along with the need for more spacious housing to accommodate us. On that trip when Callie first attempted boogie boarding, eleven of us filled a fifteen-passenger van and made the two-day trip from Abilene to South Padre. Everyone handled the trip well, and we all enjoyed time at the pool and beach and great seafood at the local restaurants. My sons-in-law and I took two mornings to rise early and fish the bay with Danny.

Throughout the leisurely week, Callie had a hard time walking, but Courtney didn't think it anything more than a toddler's occasional stumble. Phil thought it odd when he placed Callie in her car seat and she let out an unusual cry. She quickly calmed down, and he thought perhaps the car seat's metal latch heated by the summer sun had touched her leg. No one, other than her parents perhaps, grew overly concerned about Callie's behavior.

We all enjoyed a great week at South Padre. I ate enough for two men. We celebrated Carson's fourth birthday, and the beach and the fishing created new memories for our growing family. With our family tradition intact, we prepared for the two-day drive back to Abilene.

The drive home was long and the grandchildren were tired. We only stopped for meals and fuel. On one fuel stop, everyone unloaded from the van to stretch their legs. Courtney took Callie by the hand to walk inside the convenience store with Phil by her side, but Callie wouldn't walk. She only dragged her feet. Courtney looked at her husband. "Phil! Why won't she walk? What do you think's going on with her?"

Phil turned to Courtney and said, "Maybe she has an ear infection."

From an early age, Callie had middle-ear issues. When she was nine months old, she had tubes put in her ears, and repeated the procedure in March 2011. Phil scooped Callie up and carried her into the convenience store.

We arrived in San Antonio where we planned to stay the night. Callie continued to struggle with walking, and then a second issue developed. She couldn't turn her neck. We thought maybe she had developed a crick in her neck on the long drive. When Courtney brought up her concerns, she was told that it was probably nothing big. But Courtney's motherly instinct told her that wasn't the case.

Once home, my daughters and sons-in-law returned to their normal routines as Nancy and I looked forward to some peace and quiet. Except that Courtney and Phil's life wasn't back to normal. Callie's stumbling and falling grew worse. She heard an airplane, and Courtney watched as she lost her balance when she attempted to look into the sky. My granddaughter stopped climbing on the furniture and no longer made her way up the stairs. Then one day as Courtney and Callie drove home from church, Callie let out a cry from her car seat. It wasn't a normal cry, but the type of scream that said, "I'm in pain!" That did it. Callie needed to see a doctor.

Courtney pulled over to the side of the road and turned to look at her daughter. "What's wrong, Callie?"

Callie placed her hands on top of her head and screamed. Courtney grew so concerned she decided to take Callie along to Carson's scheduled checkup in hopes that Dr. Jay Capra, my close friend and grandchildren's pediatrician, could determine the source of Callie's troubling symptoms.

On the Wednesday before Father's Day, June 15, 2011, Courtney, Carson, and Callie went to Jay's office for Carson's checkup. Jay didn't know it at the time, but they weren't at the office for Carson, even though on the books it was Carson's scheduled appointment. Courtney and Phil's main concern was Callie.

Carson, a healthy, growing boy, checked out great. The only concern with Carson was an asthma issue controlled with breathing treatments. Other than that, he was the picture of health. As Jay finished Carson's checkup, Courtney expressed her ongoing concerns with Callie's stumbling and screams of pain. Jay evaluated her and found nothing wrong.

As he checked Callie, Jay asked, "How's her appetite? Has she had any nausea or vomiting?"

"She's eating well and hasn't vomited. But I can't get Callie's screaming in the car out of my mind. I think something is definitely bothering her."

Jay finished Callie's evaluation and said, "I can't find anything noticeably wrong. Let's set her up for an appointment with her ear specialist."

Courtney left Jay's office feeling a little better since he didn't seem overly concerned. The next couple of days Callie didn't worsen or improve significantly. On Friday, Courtney, Phil, Carson, and Callie traveled with Nancy to Richardson, Texas, for my nephew's graduation and for a family party after his graduation. The weekend trip was the first time Nancy had been with Callie since vacation, and she saw firsthand the stability issues which concerned Courtney.

On Father's Day Sunday, Courtney woke up and went to check on Callie. She was lying awake in her Pack 'n Play. Courtney reached down and stood Callie upright. Our granddaughter started to gag and dry heave. Fear initially gripped Courtney, but Callie quickly calmed down and Courtney relaxed, hoping it was only sinus drainage.

Everyone went downstairs for breakfast and soon prepared to head home to Abilene. After breakfast, Callie grew more and more clingy and couldn't take a step without falling.

As is often the case when trying to get ready to leave, Courtney and Phil were busy packing and taking care of two small children. They hadn't taken the time to discuss Callie's early morning episode and increased dizziness. Once in the car with everyone strapped in, Courtney and Phil shared their concerns with one another. Before pulling onto the George Bush Turnpike, Courtney said, "Let's pray this isn't something serious and that Callie will be okay."

The trip to Abilene went smoothly all the way to Eastland. Exiting off Interstate 20, Phil pulled into a restaurant parking lot. He helped Callie out of the car while Courtney took Carson's hand to walk inside to grab something to eat. Callie wasn't cooperating for Phil so Courtney turned to help. Callie began to cry and vomited onto the pavement.

After attempting to eat, everyone loaded into the car for the final hour's drive home. Courtney broke down in the car, causing Phil to ask, "Why are you so upset? Maybe it's a stomach bug."

Courtney felt otherwise. "Remember what Jay said. He asked me if Callie had issues with vomiting, and I told him no."

"Okay. What did he say to do if she started vomiting?" Phil asked with rising concern in his voice.

Courtney recalled Jay's warning. "We're to get in touch with him if she starts to throw up, because it could mean something is definitely wrong."

Callie didn't get sick the rest of the trip, until they got out of the car at home in Abilene. Callie grew worse by the hour. Nancy texted Jay to alert him to Callie's condition. Later that evening, Jay contacted Courtney to say he would schedule a CT scan for the following day.

The next day, Phil left work and met Callie and Courtney at Abilene Regional Medical Center for the CT scan. Due to her age, her parents wished for sedation for the scan, fearing the medical machinery would frighten my granddaughter, but circumstances wouldn't allow it. Her parents played lullaby music, and to their surprise, Callie remained calm. The scan was soon over, and they waited for the results.

* * * *

Nancy and I attended a funeral that morning and were eating a late lunch when my phone rang. Jay's number appeared on my screen. The call didn't last long. He had called Phil and Courtney to meet him in his office to discuss the results of the scan. My daughter and her husband would need us in the room when they received the news. We grabbed our things from the restaurant table and rushed to Jay's office. Nancy knew it was something serious, but at that time, I couldn't bear to tell her all that Jay had told me over the phone. We drove the five minutes from McAlister's Deli to Abilene Regional in silence.

We happened to pull into the parking lot at the same time as Phil and Courtney. When Courtney saw us she knew something was dreadfully wrong. I hugged her before going inside. "What's going on, Dad?" she asked. "Tell me what's wrong with Callie!"

Not wanting to speak too soon I said, "All we can do is find out and trust the Lord. Let's go inside to see what Jay has to say."

When we walked into the waiting area, Jay met us and led us back to a room. With tears in his eyes he said, "I have some terrible news. Callie has a mass on the back of her brain. It's large for a child her size. The CT scan showed the tumor to be the size of a peach. That's what is causing her dizziness, vomiting, and pain." We could barely speak. Jay explained how and when things might happen. He told Courtney that they would go to the Cook Children's Hospital's emergency room that night. Then Jay ended our brief meeting with prayer for Callie.

When Jay received the scans and report, he went into action on behalf of my granddaughter. He arranged for Callie to receive treatment at Cook Children's Hospital in Fort Worth. Jay wanted to do all he could to make sure she had the best care possible. The steps Jay took that June Monday were decisions the Lord used to protect Callie in her delicate state.

We were all in shock and were trying to keep each other going to meet the needs for the day. That meant driving to Cook Hospital and preparing for the unknown.

Phil and Courtney went home to pack clothes for Callie and themselves. Nancy and I went to our home to do the same. Courtney and Phil were in no condition to drive after receiving the news about Callie, so we packed quickly and drove to their home to pick them up. Throughout the drive, Courtney and Phil discussed some of the unknowns. New unknowns tied to my granddaughter's health replaced the old ones. The CT scan answered previous questions but raised fresh concerns.

We arrived at the emergency room and early in the process learned how the hospital for children in Fort Worth was special. The people in the emergency room took care of every need and quickly had Callie in a room for the night as nurses prepared Callie for tests the next day. The staff was great, but Callie struggled to relax. In spite of kid-friendly decorations and environment, Callie wanted her bed and her home.

On the morning of June 21, 2011, Callie underwent an additional scan. Dr. Honeycutt was the one to deliver the life-changing news to Courtney and Phil. After Emily's prayer, the room was mostly quiet. Nancy and I looked at our daughter Courtney, waiting to hear what the doctor had reported.

Courtney spoke through sobs. "Dr. Honeycutt called the tumor ependymoma. He said that the mass is the size of a peach and that they have to do surgery."

Nancy held Courtney's hand and offered a mother's voice. "Courtney, we love you. I am so sorry."

"Mom, he said the only chance for Callie to live is to remove one hundred percent of the tumor. The tumor is on the brain stem, so if the brain stem is damaged in surgery all sorts of things could happen. She might not be able to walk, talk, see, or hear. She might not even wake up." The fear of the worst-case scenario was too much for Courtney to continue.

Phil took over and described Callie's upcoming operation. He said, "The surgery could last fifteen to seventeen hours. It all depends on how attached the tumor is to the brain stem. They don't want to have to do much cutting around the brain stem because every time he cuts around the brain stem it could really hurt Callie. It also depends on how much blood Callie needs during surgery."

Others in the room asked a few questions, and then more

bad news came out. It was the question that lingered at the back of my mind. Courtney answered my question before I had the chance to ask. "Dr. Honeycutt said he is ninety-nine percent certain the tumor is malignant and that Callie will need chemo or radiation after the surgery."

Outside the consultation room friends waited, including the children's minister from Pioneer Drive Baptist Church in Abilene. Jacob went to communicate the report to them. Word spread quickly, and prayers went up instantly for Callie and for the surgery scheduled for the following day. The doctor performing Callie's surgery, Dr. David Donahue, followed up Dr. Honeycutt's visit. I can't say if the two doctors arranged the presentation format, but it appeared to me that Dr. Honeycutt came as the bad cop and Dr. Donahue came as the good cop.

Dr. Donahue brought new life to Courtney and Phil. He was the type of doctor you'd want to have perform brain surgery on your child or grandchild. He instilled a sense of confidence, but he didn't ignore the risks. However, he felt assured the surgery would go well. He gave his projected length of time for the procedure, and before he left Callie's hospital room, we held hands and prayed to our Heavenly Father for the man wielding the instruments necessary to save Callie's life. Dr. Donahue embraced the prayers, we thanked him, and a new sense of peace brought us comfort. Without question, Phil and Courtney knew the risks prior to surgery, but it calmed their fears immensely to hear from Dr. Donahue.

The next morning everyone who had stayed in the vacation house at South Padre now sat crowded together in the general waiting room. The process for Callie's surgery had begun. The night before, we took our opportunity to hug Callie, read her a story, and entertain her with toys. A rushed morning didn't allow everyone to see her prior to the surgery. Some family came to the waiting room from hotel rooms, while other family and friends made the drive from Abilene early that morning.

Friends from Phil and Courtney's church, along with Pioneer Drive's pastor, Stan Allcorn, added to the gathering of folks waiting out Callie's surgery. The group became significant enough in number that the Cook Hospital staff moved us to a private waiting area. I appreciated this, and I know Courtney did as well. Others in the general waiting room who weren't related to our group weren't dealing with such an uncertain situation, and the lighthearted manner of their behavior didn't jibe well with the tense nature of our wait.

The wait lasted roughly eight hours. Those waiting filled the time with prayer, Bible reading, school work, and encouraging conversation. Pastor Stan took Phil aside. The conversation and time together developed a stronger connection with Phil and his pastor. Courtney's friends took care of every need for the family and kept Courtney posted on how Carson's day was going. They fetched us food or coffee. At every turn, friends and spiritual encouragers stood by our family on an intensely overwhelming day.

At around three o'clock in the afternoon, a phone call came to the waiting room that the surgery was nearing an endpoint. We were all grateful to hear Callie was holding her own. Maybe thirty minutes after the phone call, Dr. Donahue marched to the center of the waiting room to tell Phil and Courtney the results of the surgery. All eyes were riveted on Callie's surgeon as we waited for his report. From his body language, I sensed a hint of pleasure in his countenance.

Dr. Donahue said, "Callie is doing really well. The procedure went much quicker than expected. It took some time to get the skin back and mark boundaries of the tumor and other important elements of the brain. Then I went for the tumor. The tumor was true to what the scans indicated. It was large for someone of Callie's age. I'm guessing she was born with it. What amazed me about the tumor was its pliable nature. It hadn't attached itself to parts of the brain except for one tiny spot on the brain stem. This isn't what I expected, since the tumor had grown near the brain stem for so long. The tumor behaved as if it was ready to come out. It pretty much fell out except for the one attachment to the brain stem. I was able to remove the entire tumor."

I turned towards Phil. We celebrated with a manly fist bump as the doctor finished his statement. When the surgeon left the room, the fist bumps turned into bear hugs. The unusual nature of the tumor was a work of God. No one expected the result. We had faith God would take care of Callie. This is what we had prayed for since we knew Callie was living in such a precarious state. The Lord heard our prayers. We expressed our deepest gratitude to the Lord. We also thanked God for Dr. Donahue, a hero by everyone's estimation. God used this man to save my granddaughter's life.

Our private waiting room at Cook's turned from a daylong vigil into an atmosphere of celebration and rejoicing. In that moment of festivity, we lacked incredible amounts of information. So many things remained unknown at 3:45 p.m. on June 22, 2011. We didn't know Callie would be unable to hear in one ear. Nor did we grasp the emotional trauma waiting for Callie in the intensive care unit as she developed an inconsolable fear of anyone wearing scrubs. And no one could predict that my granddaughter would only sleep if her mom or dad held her.

It hadn't crossed our minds that Callie's source of vital nutrition would be from a feeding tube for the next nine months. The feeding tube essentially created an umbilical-cord-like dependency between her and whoever held the backpack holding her liquid meals. At this point, on Wednesday afternoon, we had no idea Callie would endure thirty-one rounds of radiation at

MD Anderson Cancer Center in Houston. Furthermore, Phil, Courtney, and Callie would live at the hospital for forty-two days while Carson spent most of that time in Abilene.

For every terrible unknown on this journey, God provided an unforeseen blessing. We couldn't have fathomed, at that moment, the amazing ways people sought to bless my family and granddaughter by assisting financially, by keeping Carson, by taking Phil and Courtney out to supper, or by organizing a "Welcome Home" bash. We had yet to grasp fully the amazing care and support found at Cook Children's Hospital.

In that moment of celebration, we had no idea that a man sensitive to the Lord's leading would donate to the Ronald McDonald House so my family could have a room for the entire length of Callie's hospitalization.

And I couldn't have foreseen the pride I would feel when Phil and Courtney decided to bless organizations like the Ronald McDonald House and the Make-A-Wish Foundation by selling lemonade at Callie's Lemonade for a Cure Stand. We knew in the back of our minds that our church families would be a monumental presence, but hadn't expected the outpouring of love Phil and Courtney's church demonstrated when they hosted a fundraiser lunch for Callie's medical expenses.

Regardless of the unknown blessings or difficulties to come, God's Word tells us not to worry about tomorrow. We took that afternoon to celebrate God's provision for our granddaughter. Everyone in the room expressed their delight and excitement. Pastor Stan asked all of us to go to the hospital's nearby courtyard. He led us out the side doors of the waiting room to an enclosed courtyard where we reflected upon the day. The bright warm sunshine mirrored our emotions, and Pastor Stan prayed and led in a song. I felt as if the Lord had taken me to heaven. Perhaps at no other time in history has any group of people sung in such a heartfelt manner the following words:

*God is so good, God is so Good, God is so good, He's
so good to me!*

*I love Him so, I love Him so, I love Him so, He's so
good to me!*

*He answers prayer, He answers prayer, He answers
prayer, He's so good to me!*

We walked away from the courtyard with a shared conviction.
It became a mantra for Callie's battle: "Our God is so big, so
strong, and so mighty. There's nothing our God cannot do!"

9

BONE MARROW TRANSPLANT

Non-Hodgkin's lymphoma had become a way of life for me. Treating the cancer had become more complicated with the addition of PML-JC. Miraculously, the injections ordered by Dr. Greenberg kept the brain virus in remission. I still had a weakened immune system and was unsure how long the brain virus would stay at bay. We were especially unsure of the virus staying dormant when the cancer returned. The question wasn't *if* but *when* the cancer would recur. Chemotherapy could knock the cancer back, but we knew within a matter of months that it would return.

As expected, the cancer did return. After a third round of chemo, a stem cell transplant, and other various treatments, Dr. Collins recommended a bone marrow transplant. I initially refused the procedure at the time of Dr. Collins' counsel because of the risks related to the PML-JC virus. The virus was currently dormant, but one of the steps in the transplant process is to destroy what immune system remained in my body. I feared this could open the barn door wide to allow the virus to advance rapidly.

In the weeks following, I developed three criteria for possibly considering a bone marrow transplant. First, I wanted to seek the Lord's counsel through prayer. Prayer always served as a source of comfort and wisdom to me, and in this situation, it made sense to ask God for wisdom. As I prayed, a thought came to me. Had God not healed me of the PML-JC virus? And if so, did I have any reason to worry about its return?

I wanted to know the Lord's will. In times of prayer, I felt the Lord had a reason for me to live. He had brought me through numerous bouts with cancer, a brain virus, chemotherapy, and a stem cell transplant. Eventually, I knew my body would wear down from more chemo and illness. In order to live longer and serve the purposes God had for me, which I believed to be a call to share the salvation message of Jesus Christ and to love my family, I had to have a new immune system. That new immune system was available to me through a bone marrow transplant. As I prayed, a peace came over me to move forward in exploring the possibility of a bone marrow transplant.

Upon giving my consent to proceed with a transplant, my second condition was that the donor be a 100-percent match to my bone marrow. My daughters and family members were tested but no one was a close-enough match to be used as a donor. After nine months of waiting with cancer in my body, we found a donor. I learned of the donor in August 2012. My family and I thanked the Lord. We were two-thirds of the way through the criteria process. The Lord had confirmed through prayer that I should move forward and He secured a perfect match as my donor.

This gave me tremendous confidence in moving forward. Now we just had to hope that the potential donor would truly decide to donate his bone marrow and that he met my third and final criterion – he had exposure to the PML-JC virus.

If the virus was still active in my body, I wanted a new immune system that had already successfully handled the virus and developed immunity to it. Never before had a bone marrow donor received a test to determine whether exposure had occurred, but when the donor learned of the match to my body, he willingly gave more blood samples to determine if he fulfilled the third criterion. Blood tests revealed the donor had, in fact, been exposed to the PML-JC virus. The donor's immunity to the virus offered additional protection my body needed during the transplant. Since I could check off all three criteria, I decided with Nancy and the doctors to schedule the bone marrow transplant.

Cancer was growing within me, but my body managed the cancer as I waited to check in to the hospital for chemotherapy and the bone marrow transplant. The day after Nancy's birthday, December 13, 2012, we arrived at St. Paul's Hospital at UT Southwestern Transplant Center. Before our arrival, I had formed expectations as to what the hospital setup would be like. If this transplant was similar to my mother's stem cell transplant unit, I would be isolated in my room without visitors. In Mama's case, we talked to her through the window to her room but couldn't give her a hug or hold her hand for weeks. It was like being stuck in a life-size bubble that's impossible to penetrate.

St. Paul's took extensive measures to ensure their patients had limited exposure to anyone exposed to a virus recently, but the bubble was a little easier to penetrate. As a people person, I was thrilled to learn this, because five weeks without contact with my family would have made the upcoming journey very difficult.

The hospital was still unlike anything I had experienced in my previous cancer treatments or hospitalizations. My floor was only for bone marrow transplant patients. The staff served with compassion and diligence to ensure the comfort and security of each patient. Food preparation took place in a special kitchen. Anyone coming onto the floor had to wash their hands and pass a screening to enter the hallway leading to my room. After gaining entrance through the first set of locked doors, visitors had one more door to go through before entering my floor. The space between doors had a handwashing station, a mask distributor, and a camera to inspect each guest. As a patient, I looked through both sets of doors to wave to Carson, Callie, Ellie, and Ryan and tell them, "Coach loves you!"

Every bone marrow patient made the eighth floor of St. Paul's their home not for a few days but for a few weeks. I would be there for close to a month at least, while the average stay for patients was six weeks. The transplant was scheduled for December 21. I tried to settle in.

From my first day in St. Paul's, the staff proved day in and day out to be an exceptional group of nurses, dieticians, and servants. A lady came to my room several times throughout my stay to clean, and was always in a bright and pleasant mood. She cleaned up my food crumbs or spilled drinks, and tucked in my soft, brown blanket so it wouldn't fall off the bed during the night. Most importantly, she welcomed conversation about faith in Christ and my grandchildren. We became friends, which was a blessing in a place like this where you needed every friend possible.

At one point, my new friend hadn't come to clean for a couple of days in a row. I asked a floor nurse if everything was okay. The nurse informed me that the arthritis in my room cleaner's knee occasionally flared up and that she really needed surgery. When I heard this, it humbled me to see how joyfully and diligently she had performed her job even with a throbbing knee.

I also developed a friendship with a new doctor, a bone marrow transplant specialist, who worked under Dr. Collins' supervision. Dr. Prapti Patel came to my room every morning to inform me of blood counts and the medical process. I lifted my shirt every time she came to examine the trifusion, which consisted of two additional lines and my port. If any infection developed around these areas, it would delay the start of my transplant. I tested out well and my blood counts were holding up.

The first couple of days the doctors ran more blood work and prepared my body for a final round of chemo in preparation for the pending bone marrow transplant. Dr. Collins came in and presented me with his dilemma. He had to decide which chemotherapy to use to treat the cancer and eliminate my immune system. He described the chemo possibilities by using a sledgehammer as an analogy.

"Dale, we can use a five-pound, ten-pound, or twenty-pound sledgehammer on your body. The twenty-pound sledgehammer could potentially weaken your body so significantly that you might die. The ten-pound or five-pound hammer might not be strong enough to eliminate your immune system, so a problem might arise in transplanting the donor's bone marrow. Then when the cancer returned this would have all been for naught. You and I need to pray about this decision. I'll pray tonight. Tomorrow I'll let you know what I think is best. We need to strike a delicate balance."

I appreciated Dr. Collins' desire to take this very important decision to the Lord in prayer. Nancy and I trusted our Heavenly Father would give him the wisdom to make the best decision for my health and treatment.

The next morning Dr. Collins told me he chose the ten-pound hammer. While that course wouldn't be a walk in the park, it wouldn't be as hard on my body as the twenty-pound hammer. Roughly ten days of chemotherapy followed. With previous chemo treatments, I would arrive at the hospital, take chemo, and return to civilization. This wasn't the case with this round of chemo. It was administered in my room, and there were no plans for me to leave. For the next twenty-three days, I was in a healthcare prison. I didn't leave the floor.

Family and friends came by; a kindness that made the days

pass a little quicker. Even friends from my days at North Garland High and McMurry University stopped by for a visit. Seeing them after so many years reminded me that even friends not seen in decades were supporting me.

The nurses also became a source of companionship. I made it my daily goal to be the patient who made my nurses' job more enjoyable. I thought about how difficult their job must be in seeing the trying circumstances of every patient day-in and day-out. In some cases, they had to care for people who would never leave the hospital alive.

A board located at the nurses' station listed the name of each patient followed by a number at the end of the patient's row. The number indicated how many days the patient could expect to stay at St. Paul's before moving to an apartment or hotel for daily visits to his or her doctor. It saddened me greatly when a name was erased from the board prematurely. I understood it was part of their job to see patients die, but it couldn't be easy on them. Special bonds are formed on the eighth floor of St. Paul's, and in light of the staff's sacrifice and dedication, I tried to create an environment in my room of light and life.

The nurses, doctors, Nancy, and I became family and found ways to laugh and lighten the mood. During the first week of my stay, when I felt decent, Jacob, Emily, and Ellie planned to visit. Nancy went down to the first floor to meet my daughter and her family since Ellie wasn't allowed on the floor.

I had arranged with one of my caregivers to have a little fun with Jacob and Emily. When they came through the first set of double doors, the nurse viewed my family through the camera and gave instructions via the intercom to Jacob and Emily. It was set up so we could see and hear them, but my daughter and son-in-law only heard the nurse.

The nurse said, "Hello, Emily. Your Dad is excited to see

y'all, but before you come in, I need to ask you to first wash your hands." They did as instructed.

"Thank you. Now, I need to ask you a few questions. Have you had a fever in the last forty-eight hours or had contact with a person who has a fever or infection?"

"No, we haven't," they answered.

"Wonderful. Now we need to engage in a few screening exercises," my partner in crime continued. "First, will you please raise your hands in the air?" Emily and Jacob looked oddly at one another but raised their hands in the air.

"Good. Everything looks fine. Now, with your hands in the air, please turn around in a full circle." The subjects of our prank turned a full 360 degrees, returning to face the camera. By this time I was laughing hard, and I have to say I'm not sure how the nurse could talk without cracking up.

I said to the nurse, "Tell them you need to see the bottoms of their shoes."

The nurse played the part perfectly, employing a professional tone. "Thank you, Emily and Jacob. We have a few more steps to ensure the safety of the patients on this floor. Now, will you please lift both shoes towards the camera so I can inspect the bottoms of your shoes? You may have stepped in a piece of chewed gum or dog ..., well, you know, before you came into the hospital."

My good-natured daughter and son-in-law may have gotten suspicious at this point but turned their backs to the camera so the camera could see the bottoms of their shoes. By this time, at least ten nurses and other staff had gathered around the camera, laughing hysterically.

"Thank you. Everything looks clean." I gave the final instruction, and my friend repeated it into the microphone.

"Now, Jacob, this one is for you only. Would you please lift your shirt in order to check for any unusual rashes?" That was it. The prank was over.

Jacob eyed the camera suspiciously. "What's going on?"

I stepped around the corner doubled over in laughter and waved at Emily. The nurse hit the control button and the doors opened. The close-to-a-dozen hospital staff, who had gotten quite a kick out of this, greeted Jacob and Emily. They seemed as excited as I was to see my family. Their enthusiasm demonstrated how, in a short time, we had become like family – a family that needed a good laugh.

The nurses and I found other things to laugh about, but we also became comfortable enough with one another to the point where we shared burdens as patient to nurse and nurse to patient. With the development of this mutual trust, they shared some of their own personal struggles with me. On one visit to my room, I commented to the nurse about my ministry and calling to minister to cancer patients. This one statement launched an incredible ministry opportunity. Word spread among the nurses about my ministry. I offered encouragement and prayer. I prayed for ill children, life decisions, and renewed walks with God.

The nurses took it upon themselves to gain permission from neighboring patients to share their stories with me. If a patient agreed, I eagerly went to their room for prayer and conversation. I asked God to use me to be a spark of hope to each patient.

In the middle of my second week of chemo, the nurse asked if I would make a visit to a young lady down the hall. The nurse informed me the patient lived in the Big Country near Abilene and would like to meet me. When the nurse gave me the patient's information, only a short window of time existed to make the visit before one of us would be physically unable to visit. I agreed and planned to visit before lunch. My best time of the day physically came in the daytime, and I wanted to make sure the visit happened while I was at my peak physically.

I walked into the patient's room. Upon seeing her on her bed, I tried to hold my composure. Out of all the visits I have made to hospital rooms, this visit remains one of the most difficult. Lying on the bed was a young lady perhaps in her early twenties. She was missing her right arm and left leg. After introducing myself, a relative in the room informed me that the amputee had undergone several surgeries and battled cancer on multiple occasions. The young girl didn't say much, but the state of her body said it all. She was my youngest daughter's age. Instead of experiencing the fun of youth, she was laying in a hospital room with an uncertain future.

I turned my attention to the patient and said, "Hi, I'm Dale. How are you today?"

"I'm doing well. Thank you for stopping by." The warmth in her voice told me she meant what she said.

Our conversation turned to what we had in common. We were cancer survivors facing a bone marrow transplant (BMT). It surprised me how much enthusiasm she had for the upcoming procedure. With so many handy excuses to live in a state of pity, she demonstrated remarkable strength. When I had my port insert years ago, I remember feeling elated that it wasn't on my right side, which would have prevented me from being able to shoot a rifle. My celebration all seemed a little silly now when this girl didn't even have an arm.

Before our conversation ended, I let her know how much she inspired me and that I would pray for her every day. The smile across her face touched my heart. I prayed a calm, typical prayer. I returned to my room for a bolder, more passionate plea to the Lord. As is the case with most people I met on the BMT floor, I have no idea how her transplant went, but I faithfully prayed asking God to heal her and for me to have the kind of joy she showed during our visit.

Along with all the visits, I also wanted to prepare my body for the bone marrow transplant by exercising and working out. The transplant unit had a workout room with a treadmill and some hand weights. I went every day to the workout room to walk and jog on the treadmill. Exercise provided a mental escape from my surroundings. I pretended I was on a walk from the lake house cabin to the old green cabin passing through the triple gates before nearing the south end of the orchard. In my mind, I then navigated the cattle guard before meandering by my parents' green cabin. I finally ventured onto the county road shaded by a canopy of towering oaks. Pressing the stop button, I stepped off the treadmill to do pushups. It's hard to imagine anything while performing pushups.

I impressed the nurses, Dr. Patel, and Dr. Collins with my energy and determination. They were accustomed to patients who stuck to their rooms and demonstrated all the expected conditions of a weary cancer patient. With my workouts, I entered a pushup competition with Dr. Collins. During every consultation, I proudly shared my number for the day knowing he had performed more than I had. My last workout was extremely difficult as I pushed myself all the way to twenty-five pushups. This doesn't sound like very many, but each pushup worked my mental will as much as anything physical.

Eventually, Dr. Collins ended the pushup challenge. He said, "You need to stop the workouts and rest up for the transplant."

After the first week, the workouts had required more energy and work than when I first entered the hospital, so I decided not to protest his advice. Less strenuous activity would have to fill my days.

My hospital stay gave me the opportunity to join the technological world. Nancy had used a tablet for quite some time.

In fact, it hardly left her side. I joked with her that the tablet was her new boyfriend because he took up quite a bit of her attention. Nevertheless, Nancy believed having a tablet would be a good way for me to pass the time. I enjoyed the games my new "girlfriend" offered. I read news and learned how to text. My daughters, quite savvy with the technological world, had texted their mom often, and now I was able to join in. I couldn't type very well, however, and had to rely on the voice automation to type out my texts.

These voice-automated messages ended up giving Nancy and my daughters a good laugh. That's because I didn't quite understand how the technology worked. I thought the voice automation would accurately text what I spoke. I didn't realize how mightily my tablet struggled to understand my Texas accent. More often than not, the final version of the text was a scrambled version of what I intended to send. After receiving several smiley faces, LOLs, and confused responses, I began to proofread and edit before sending my digital messages.

I had hours to type thoughts and reflections onto the electronic notepad, so I also used the tablet to write down memories to be shared with Nancy and the girls. I recorded some of my favorite sayings and teachings. I read Scripture from the apps Nancy installed and recorded my reflections. I even had an app that read Scripture to me. In lonely times, it became a companion of sorts.

Of course, the tablet could never replace a human presence, especially Nancy's. No one could comfort me like she did. We talked, laughed, prayed, and reflected upon the future. She helped me stay positive and knew exactly what kind of medicines and treatment I was to receive. Nancy has always understood exactly what I needed and when. She was my helpmate, my companion, and the person who stayed with me throughout this whole process and beyond.

Ten days after my admittance into St. Paul's Hospital, I woke up ready – ready to begin a process God had repeatedly confirmed was the path to take. Nancy, my father, Keith, Jacob, and Emily gathered in the room to encourage me and pray. One by one, we went around the room and prayed for God to use the transplant to bring complete healing to my body.

We were all curious about how my body would respond and what would transpire during the transplant process. The bone marrow arrived during the night, transported in a special cooler. My healthcare plan paid for two airline tickets: one for the courier and one for the cooler.

Without fanfare, the nurse suddenly appeared in my room clutching the Styrofoam container – my new bone marrow. We all acted like she was carrying precious, valuable cargo, because she was. The cooler contained several bags of bone marrow in case of malfunction or loss. Dr. Collins wanted to have extra bone marrow in case the need for a second transplant arose in the future. The spare bone marrow would be stored at a blood bank.

The nurse overseeing the transplant took the bone marrow from the cooler and held my new life in her hands. Without hesitation, I asked her to place the bone marrow in my hands. The bag resembled most plastic IV bags. Inside of it, the bone marrow looked like a cherry slush. My thoughts turned to how the Bible tells us that life is in the blood of Jesus. My spiritual salvation is secure in Christ's blood; now I desired new life physically. I examined the bag and thought, "Is this what God will use to save my life?"

The nurse initiated preparations. She used an instrument that looked like a razor handle with a gauze pad on the end to apply a chemical much stronger than alcohol to clean all the different pieces used in the transplant. She moved with great care, ensuring every connection, line, and skin around the trifusion lines used to receive the bone marrow were completely sterilized.

After what felt like an hour of preparation, my body began to receive the transplant. I declared December 21, 2012, to be my third birthday. The day I was born served naturally as my first birthday. The second birthday was a spiritual birth upon receiving Christ as my savior at age seven. My bone marrow transplant served as my third birthday.

In the week before my transplant, Dr. Patel made a joke about my transplant day sharing the calendar with what Mayan Indians believed to be the date the world would end. According to the Mayan calendar, the world was supposed to end on December 21, my transplant day. A significant amount of tabloid speculation and media coverage had raised the public's awareness of the ancient belief.

I replied to her, kidding, "Dr. Patel, the world can't end December 21, 2012, because that's the day God is giving me new life!"

We both laughingly agreed, but it was another event that uniquely connected events and dates in my life.

The decisive moment finally arrived. The nurse initiated the flow of bone marrow from the bag through the tube towards my body. The red, lava-like flow inched closer to my body. If I had any reservations about this, it was too late to do anything about it now. The prayer now was that my body would receive the new life without extreme complications like cardiac arrest. Everyone watched me as if I was a fifth-grade scientific experiment seconds from eruption.

The first few days following the bone marrow transplant went relatively well. I laid on a hospital bed miles away from family and home. My body's immunity prevented me from walking out of the wing, much less walking outside to observe a sunny winter day. I missed feeling the sunshine on my face and the touch of a cool breeze. Instead, the only interaction I had with nature was from my window as I peered outside to look at the world on the other side of the glass.

For six weeks, I didn't eat at restaurants, attend a business lunch, or attend church. I stayed in the box of the eighth floor at St. Paul's Hospital. When Nancy or the kids left, I walked to the end of the hallway to a window that overlooked the parking lot. We waved and blew kisses before they got in their car. If Courtney, Malory, or Emily happened to be in the passenger seat, we watched each other as their vehicle turned onto the street, veered onto the highway, and then disappeared under the overpass. This provided two more minutes of being together. After that last glance, I was alone.

I did the same thing with Nancy as she left Christmas Eve for our family celebration in Abilene. Since the bone marrow transplant occurred four days before Christmas, Nancy returned to Abilene to have Christmas with the kids and grandchildren. The house had no tree or lights, but this didn't diminish the Christmas spirit and the joy that comes in celebrating the birth of Christ. Missing Christmas with family at home was difficult. I love family gatherings, but I drew comfort from the knowledge that receiving the bone marrow transplant would allow me to enjoy many more Christmases to come.

With the help of technology, I didn't totally have to miss out on Christmas morning with my family. I watched live as my daughters and their families exchanged gifts in our family living room. Occasionally one of my daughters or sons-in-law looked to the camera and exchanged a brief word of conversation. A couple times the Internet connection failed, and I had to figure out, without Nancy's assistance, how to get the connection back. But I did it! And watching the grandkids enjoy Christmas definitely lifted my spirits.

The view on my tablet's screen took me to nostalgic Christmas memories when my girls were young and received gifts from Santa. I thought of the time Santa left a trampoline in the front yard, and Courtney, being old enough to understand, looked at Nancy and me with an "I can't believe you did this for us" stare. The girls spent hours jumping on that trampoline and attempted to spend several nights camping out on it before coyote howls sent them scampering into the security of the house.

That Christmas in the hospital, I also had a little holiday fun of my own with those who had left their families at home to care for my medical needs on Christmas day. Knowing I would be in the hospital on Christmas day, Nancy packed my jolly-red suit and hat for the occasion. For several years, I enjoyed dressing up as Santa Claus and arriving at where my daughters taught school to let the boys and girls share their wish lists with Santa. I had dropped some weight and didn't fill out the suit as I once did. Nonetheless, I yanked the suit out of my bag and pulled on the red pants, red coat, and boots. I put my Santa hat and white beard on and walked towards the nursing station with a loud "HO, HO, HO! Merry Christmas!"

I took the crowd by complete surprise. The nurses were beside themselves with excitement. I gave them all candy canes, wished them a Merry Christmas, made conversation, visited a few patient rooms, and returned to my room. My St. Paul's family Christmas was complete.

Celebrating Christmas with my family and hospital staff turned out to be a day of peace and joy, before the full strength of the transplant's wrath hit me. The day after Christmas brought a wave of difficulties. I thank the Lord Nancy returned to the hospital on December 26. I needed her calming presence. Throughout the next several days, my body faced affliction every waking minute as effects from the bone marrow transplant tormented it.

In the days prior to the transplant, I wondered how and when my body would begin to change. On December 26, I received my answer. I started to feel pain in my bones and joints. The nurse tried to encourage me by saying, "This is a positive sign. It means the transplant is working."

I repeated her bubbly encouragement over and over to myself as the pain intensified. It started in my shoulders and moved through my back, hips, legs, and feet.

This was, unfortunately, only the beginning. The next four to five days proved to be the most challenging of my entire stay in the hospital. I woke up on December 26 feeling fair, but the pain continued to increase throughout the day. By nighttime, it was like a hammer's strike against every inch of my body with each heartbeat. The nurses administered heavy doses of morphine, and a massage therapist visited every day to help ease the residual soreness I experienced.

I repeated this process for the next three days and reached the pinnacle of pain on December 29. The hammer's strike against my body started earlier in the day than the previous three days. I had a saying with the girls that sometimes you had to fake it, if you had to, so wipe off your sad face. Several times throughout my health battles, I had successfully faked it with visitors, including Nancy and my daughters. But on the eighth day after my transplant, I couldn't fake it any longer. In the four days since Christmas, I had lost my appetite and relied on IV hydration. Nancy normally slept in the hospital basement, in rooms once dedicated to nuns, but the last several nights she stayed with me and rubbed my hands and feet as the pain intensified exponentially. I cried out in pain as my joints and muscles cramped in response to the invading bone marrow. The strength and willpower needed to make it from my bed to the bathroom vanished.

I am a person who never gives up. If we needed one more stop in the fourth quarter, one more pass with a rake, or one more ounce of strength to keep one of my work hands on the ground as we wrestled at the workday's end, I could muster it. But now, for the first time in my life, I was ready to have it all end. I had spent everything I had in regards to will, stamina, and resolve. Unapologetically, I couldn't do it. I was comfortable with death and said so to God.

Fortunately, I made it through that night to a calmer day. As 2013 approached, the pain gradually subsided. My overall attitude improved. I tried to understand all the affliction, looking at it as a way the Lord was trying to teach me. The psalmist wrote: *It is **good** for me that I have been afflicted; that I might learn thy statutes* (Psalm 119:71).

The week from Christmas to New Year's Day proved to be brutal, but after the most difficult days, I started to feel great improvement. Visitors provided immense encouragement and distracted me from the confinement of my hospital room. I was grateful for each visit and the effort friends and family made to see me. Above all, the prayers lifted up to our Heavenly Father on my behalf were a tremendous source of power and comfort.

As I continued to improve, Dr. Collins said that my body's reception of the transplant was proceeding terrifically. I wasn't the best bone marrow transplant recipient ever, but I was in the top ninety-five percent. I was also apparently ahead of schedule in regards to length of stay. The average BMT stay is six weeks. I would transition to a nearby apartment after only four weeks following my admittance to St. Paul's hospital.

On January 6, 2013, Nancy and I gathered our belongings from my temporary hospital home and prepared to move to the next interim home. The temporary home was a nice two-bedroom apartment near the hospital, making it convenient for daily evaluations by my healthcare team. We enjoyed cooking our own meals and walking outside anytime I felt like it. Dr. Collins wanted me to take integrating back into large groups of people like restaurants or malls very slowly. Overall, I had to be extremely careful about what I ate and what I exposed myself to due to my very weak immune system.

We stayed in the apartment without returning home for close to a month. Our children came to visit along with several friends. When my daughters came for a visit, they still had to leave our grandchildren behind to prevent exposure to a potential illness that would land me back in the hospital.

The apartment complex had a relaxing courtyard with a Ping-Pong table. It wasn't quite the same as racquetball, which I loved, but it helped me build strength in my leg and arm muscles. It only took one match of Ping-Pong to drain my energy. Then I'd have to go back to the apartment and rest. Considering my lack of strength, some of my friends and sons-in-law's pride took a hit when a transplant patient beat them at Ping-Pong. Sometimes they'd claim they "let me win" out of sympathy. Nancy and I played many games, and she won her fair share. I kept that information mostly hidden from my sons-in-law to protect their egos.

In the month following my release from St. Paul's, I steadily gained strength. Dr. Collins monitored my health closely. I took several medicines on a precise schedule. Nancy and I set several alarms so I wouldn't forget my Prograf medicine that controlled graft-versus-host disease, which affects many bone marrow transplant patients. Some of the alarms sounded like ambulance sirens. While Nancy and I were accustomed to the alarms, they were more than slightly unnerving to our guests when they visited.

While I was doing well, in the back of my mind I knew there were no guarantees that the bone marrow transplant would work. My body could completely reject the transplant, even though the odds were slim. Or, with my wiped-out immune system, I could catch something like the flu and grow very ill.

I was thankful that complications due to the BMT, aside from the four-day stretch of hammer-pounding pain in the hospital, were minimal. I tried to see each day as a tremendous gift from God. I believed then and believe now that the Lord will sustain me. According to Psalm 145, the Lord's place is to uphold and raise up. He definitely acted in this way on my behalf.

* * * *

On February 15, I finally saw the city of Dallas in my rear-view mirror as we headed to Abilene and on to Lubbock to celebrate the arrival of Malory's first baby, Addison Marie Foster. I couldn't wait to see my fifth grandchild. The Lord had brought me through a severe health battle to enjoy special moments such as this with my family.

We arrived in Lubbock that evening and tried to settle in to get some rest. We knew the next day would be a full twenty-four hours. Nancy left early on Addison's birthday to enjoy time with Courtney, Emily, and our soon-to-be mother. Later in the afternoon, I received word from Nancy to load up the kids and drive to the hospital. Addison was moments from making a splash into our lives.

Phil, Jacob, and I headed to the hospital where we corralled the kids in the waiting room of University Medical Center. Carson knew what was happening, but I'm not sure about the other three children. When they heard Addison cry on the other side of the door, they wanted to see the baby and didn't really want to wait an hour to meet their new cousin.

When I held our granddaughter, I felt as if I was holding the same little baby as when I held our third daughter over two decades earlier. She looked exactly like Malory did when she was born. Addison caught everyone's eye with a head full of long, black hair. She could have easily worn a bow that first day of her life. For the first time in several months, we all gathered in one room. I circled everyone together for prayer; my family and I rejoiced in the moment. After leaving Malory, Steve, and our new granddaughter, Addison, Nancy and I returned to the Dallas apartment where we lived until the end of March.

Before returning to Abilene to settle in to life back home, Dr. Collins made sure he had my attention. He knew my former work ethic and the full schedule I kept. To make his point, Dr. Collins told me about a man who left Dallas to return home in even better condition than mine. Once home, the man returned to working in his shop cutting and sanding wood. Tragically, the little sawdust he inhaled was enough to create an infection in his lungs leading to the man's death. Dr. Collins' story hit the mark. I took it easy but had to rein in my sizeable ambition to get back to the things I enjoyed doing before the transplant – like playing a game of racquetball, moving dirt, or visiting men and women fighting cancer.

Despite following doctor's orders, my blood counts were low, and I needed a blood transfusion immediately. Dr. Collins decided I should receive the blood in Abilene, but I had concerns about doing this in a hospital that didn't take the same precautions as the dedicated wing of St. Paul's used in their operation.

Moments after receiving the blood, I had a reaction to the transfusion. My body began to reject it. I experienced full-body convulsions and felt my airway constricting. I told Nancy to notify the girls. I was unsure how the situation would unfold, but eventually, with medication, my body calmed down.

Aside from these two main flare-ups and several minor annoyances to my comfort, we enjoyed dinners with friends we hadn't seen in some time. Every worship service or Bible study group I attended at our church made me feel more connected to life prior to the bone marrow transplant.

I slowly entered back into work and missions involvement.

Nancy and I scheduled times for missionaries to come to our home and share their ministry with area churches. We planned a family trip to Ruidoso, New Mexico, for the summer. Because of my transplant, I had to be very careful with sun exposure, and my family all agreed that the annual trip to South Padre would have to wait for another year as we traded the warm, sun-soaked beaches for the cooler mountains.

We left for Ruidoso on Father's Day, June 15, 2013. It felt great to celebrate the day with all my girls. We rented a three-story cabin near a golf course. The cool mornings brought relief from the summer heat in Texas, which quickly drained my energy level.

During the week, we played spades at the cabin and ventured out to enjoy Dollar Hot Dog Day at the Ruidoso Downs Race Track. The kids loved the horses. We also enjoyed a seafood buffet at the restaurant near the horse track... It was no match for Louie's Backyard in South Padre, but we did the best with what we had.

The highlight of the week was our evening at the Flying J Ranch. Friends had recommended this place to us as a great scene for family fun. We loaded up in three vehicles and headed towards the ranch. That night I felt like Coach again. I chased our five grandkids through teepees, took them on pony rides, and sifted for play gold. We took in a staged gunfight, fetched cups of butter pecan ice cream, danced to western tunes, and laughed with Ellie and Callie as a singer in the band broke out into a yodel.

Day by day, life and my health became more as I remembered it before cancer, before the brain virus, and before the bone marrow transplant. I started to exercise, play racquetball, and schedule appointments with men who were searching for faith or encouragement for the faith already within them. Yet in the months following the bone marrow transplant, I had an unmet goal. I wanted to stay healthy and alive so that at the one-year anniversary of my bone marrow transplant I could receive my donor's information and make contact with a real-life hero. My thoughts and prayers had been with the man who gave a part of his life to save mine. I greatly anticipated the moment when I, along with my family, could communicate our gratitude.

10

WELCOME TO TEXAS

Shawn Wilson, an Abilene airport employee and friend, boarded the small American Airlines plane at the gate to make an announcement. Passengers on the plane included Jeff, Krista, Kelly, and Robin Babbitt from a suburb near Seattle, Washington.

Shawn made his announcement. "Ladies and Gentlemen, I am pleased to welcome Jeff Babbitt and his family all the way from Washington State. Jeff gave his bone marrow to save an Abilene man's life, and they are about to meet for the first time inside the airport. Ladies and Gentlemen, please help me welcome Jeff Babbitt to Abilene, Texas."

Shawn later told me how the passengers gave Jeff and his family a great Texas welcome with a loud round of applause. Jeff turned to his family and said, "Let's go in and meet some really nice people."

Nancy and I stood eagerly awaiting our guests on the airport's first floor. Two of my daughters and their kids joined us and a newspaper photographer and a local news station waited to capture the sights and sounds of our first meeting. I had met several important people at the Abilene airport in my lifetime. Previously, we had welcomed Brother Abraham and his wife from India, and Jacques and Marie Alexandre from Haiti. As much as I love those people and others, I experienced a completely different assortment of emotions as I prepared to meet the man God used to give me new life physically.

Carson, Callie, Ellie, and Ryan pressed their faces to the glass wall of the escalator. Folks descending the escalator smiled and waved for the camera. We waited with anticipation for Jeff and his family to appear. Then we spotted them at the landing one floor above us, and without exaggerating, I can say Jeff and I looked so much alike that we could have passed for brothers.

* * * *

In the fall of 2009, Jeff was out of work. He had honorably served in the United States Marine Corps. After serving our country, he found work as a truck driver. His most recent employer went through a round of layoffs, and the company cut Jeff's job. Fortunately, Jeff's wife, Krista, had a job at a local hospital near Seattle. Their daughters were eight and six years old at the time.

One night during this time of not having a day-to-day job, Krista told Jeff of a blood drive that the hospital had scheduled for the next day. She wondered if Jeff wanted to come to the hospital, give blood, and then have lunch together. Jeff agreed and looked forward to the opportunity to have lunch with his wife.

The next morning, he made the drive to the hospital and prepared to donate blood. While registering to donate, the attendant working the blood drive asked if Jeff had ever heard of the bone marrow donor database. He hadn't. She asked if he would be willing to sign up. In her appeal she said, "The chances of ever receiving a call to donate your bone marrow are astronomically small, but you never know. You might be called to save a life."

Jeff not only gave blood but also registered to become a bone marrow donor. After registering, he really didn't think about the actual possibility of donating. However, a few years later, Jeff received the phone call he never expected. A person from the bone marrow registry shared the news that he was a potential match along with nine other people. The person on the phone asked Jeff to come to the blood bank for further testing to determine who among the ten people would be the best match.

The results of the tests came back, and Jeff received a second phone call. He was the perfect fit, a 100-percent match for a man in need of a bone marrow transplant. The blood bank employee asked Jeff if he was still willing to donate, and he eagerly committed to the donation process. They explained that a date hadn't been determined yet, because it all depended on the health of the recipient and whether or not the procedure would actually take place.

A year passed and Jeff received a third phone call. Everything was good to go. The recipient was ready, if he still agreed to donate his bone marrow. Without hesitating, Jeff agreed and put December 20, 2012, on his calendar. On this day, he took a day off from work to potentially save the life of a person he had never met. He went into the hospital for the extraction of his bone marrow, almost completely blind as to who was to receive it.

They administered a few injections prior to the donation process. Then the time came to donate. Nurses hooked him up to a special bone marrow extraction machine. It pumped his bone marrow into several bags for transport to the recipient's location. A nurse unhooked the bags and placed Jeff's bone marrow in a cooler. A few minutes later, a lady walked in to collect the cooler and left for the airport to catch a plane to Dallas, Texas.

* * * *

Nineteen hundred miles away and months before this flight, I hoped for a call from a lady by the name of Christen Bennett. As the transplant coordinator from UT Southwestern, she would call to update me on the status of the hospital's search for a bone marrow donor. Finally, one day she called to inform Nancy and me that they had secured a potential bone marrow donor. This was a hallelujah of hallelujahs.

After the bone marrow transplant, if I maintained good health for a year, Christen would also be the person to call with my donor's contact information. A year later and a few days after Christmas (which I gladly celebrated at home instead of in the bone marrow ward), Christen called with a name and phone number. I wrote the information on a notepad and hung up the phone. I looked at the name, Jeffrey Babbitt from Washington State. I stared at his name and this time I thanked the Lord for my donor by name.

I had so many reasons for my gratitude in regards to Jeff. While without a job, he decided to give blood. Giving blood led to registering as a potential bone marrow donor. Registering as a bone marrow donor led to an actual request for his bone marrow. Jeff willingly gave a few hours of his life in hopes that it would save my life. Jeff later told me that he went home after donating and prayed for me as my body prepared to receive his bone marrow.

I wanted to call right away. However, I decided to call on New Year's Day. There would be no better way to start 2014. Courtney, Emily, and their families would be at the house for a New Year's Day supper. I slated that as the best time to call so my family could join in the conversation. My thoughts and prayers turned towards that moment. In the conversation, I hoped that Jeff would sense the depth of our sincere gratitude and the love we had for him and his family.

On January 1, 2014, my family began to arrive at our home. I was glad to see everyone, but found myself preoccupied with how the phone call would go. Part of me wondered if we would even be able to reach Jeff with the number Christen gave me.

After everyone arrived, we gathered around the table to call Jeff. The younger grandkids played nearby, but Carson, my oldest grandson, was intrigued with the call and found an open spot around the table and joined us. I felt butterflies in my stomach as I picked up the phone and dialed Jeff's number.

My emotions ran high. I wondered if I could hold it together when Jeff answered the phone. I didn't have much time to think about it though.

"Hello."

"Jeffrey Babbitt, please."

"This is him." The man who the Lord used to save my life was on the line.

"Jeffrey Babbitt, this is Dale Morrison in Abilene, Texas. How are you doing today?"

"Well, I am fine. Do I know you?"

"Jeffrey, you probably know me," I said trying to keep my voice strong. It was a losing battle. "I am the one you saved when you gave your bone marrow to help me."

Jeff told me later that when he heard those words he knees buckled. It had been quite some time since he'd donated his bone marrow, and he had given permission to share his information months earlier. He figured that whoever received his bone marrow had either died or had declined to learn his identity. Based on his assumptions, Jeff had moved on and didn't expect a call.

Now at the other end of the call, he searched for words. "I'm speechless. I'm thrilled I was able to do that for you."

"Yeah, I understand being speechless. You did a wonderful

thing, and my family is sitting around the table to say hello to you and your family."

"How long has it been since the transplant?" Jeff asked.

I replied, "It's been a year, man."

"Unbelievable."

"So, thank you for allowing me to get your number and call you. I just wondered if you had a few minutes I would like to visit with you."

The call clearly overwhelmed Jeff as he attempted to take everything in. "So everything went fine?" he asked.

"Jeffrey, it worked amazingly well. The Lord just really blessed me. Several months went by when they couldn't find a donor for me. I had fought cancer for five years, and then I got the JC virus in the brain. I think I got it when I went to Haiti to do some mission relief work after the earthquake."

I shared with Jeff what the doctor said about my need for a donor and the process I went through in deciding whether to receive a BMT. I told him I prayed about it, thought about it, but didn't receive a peace about proceeding with the transplant until I learned of Jeff.

"So a young lady at UT Southwestern contacted me. Her name is Christen Bennett. She's the one who called me a few days ago with your number. I decided to wait until today to call, because I thought it would be very appropriate with today being the first day of 2014. Thank you."

Jeff tried to shake off the overwhelming shock. "I'm numb and speechless. I had wondered if I would find out. We are getting ready to watch the game tonight, and wow. You called."

"Well, you did a beautiful thing. I love you like a brother, and I don't even know you."

Jeff answered, "Thank you."

"So, anyway, you were a one-hundred percent match. When Christen came to my wife and me and said this is a one-hundred percent match and that the donor matches my body to a T in every area, that's when the Lord gave me peace and we decided to go forward. You see, as I prayed about this, Jeff, I thought, 'Well, if the Lord provides somebody that matches perfectly with me, I'll do it. I'll take the risk even if there was a chance of death.'"

"When I committed to the transplant, I thought perhaps you might back out when you heard that you would need to donate and go through the shots around Thanksgiving and Christmas. I prayed you would be able to stick with it. They never told me about you personally, but they did tell me about all you would go through to prep for it."

"Well, Dale, it was no problem, and I will do it again if I need to."

"Thank you, Jeff. Thank you for saving my life."

Filled to the brim with emotion and holding back tears, I asked Jeff if he had time to visit with my family. Nancy, Carson, Courtney, and Emily took a turn expressing their gratitude and appreciation. As each one talked to Jeff, the main theme was "thank you." Nancy said, "Thank you for saving my husband." My girls each said, "Thank you for saving my Daddy." Carson said, "Thank you for saving my Coach."

When Jacob asked why Jeff had decided to register as a donor, we learned about how Jeff had been out of work at the time, how he planned to donate blood, and then have lunch with his wife. As Jeff heard from each of my family members, I'm confident he felt the impact of his actions upon my life and family.

Before ending the conversation, I expressed my family's desire to welcome Jeff and his family to Abilene. "We would enjoy the opportunity to get to know you and to thank you face to face."

Jeff expressed his appreciation for the invitation and said, "I would love to come."

I also shared my hope that he and I could host a health fair where we could give people the opportunity to do the same thing he did for me. He was all in and gave me his full affirmation.

In the weeks after Jeff and I spoke on the phone that New Year's Day, Nancy and I worked on a health fair planned for June. We secured Pioneer Drive Baptist Church as the location. Restaurants agreed to help by providing food. I must have gone to more than twenty restaurants and everyone agreed to donate food or beverages for the event.

In our work for this event, I sought to have an opportunity for people to register as potential bone marrow donors and organ donors. I also wanted to have a blood drive at the health fair. I contacted the respective organizations and all agreed to attend. I later learned that the health fair Jeff and I hosted was the first time that Be The Match, Donate Life Texas, and Meek Blood Center were all at the same health event in Abilene. We set the date for June 28, 2014, and used every media outlet available to let people know about the event.

Two days before the health fair, Jeff and Krista descended the airport escalator with their two daughters. When they reached the first floor, I stuck out my hand, shook his hand, and gave him a one-armed bear hug. "Jeff, welcome to Texas. I am so glad you came."

"Thank you. We're happy to be here with you," Jeff said.

"I'm glad you didn't turn around and head back to Washington when you saw all the cameras. I didn't want to overwhelm you. We could have had a lot more people here because so many of our friends wanted to meet you."

We introduced our wives and daughters. Nancy, Krista, and our girls visited as I brought Carson over to meet Jeff. "Jeff, this is Carson. He would like to present you with a special cap to wear everywhere you go while you're in Abilene."

Carson shook Jeff's hand and handed him a Texas Rangers baseball cap. Jeff attempted to place it on his head, but the cap was a little small. After adjusting it, he placed it back on his head and wore the blue cap with the white Texas Rangers "T" the rest of the evening.

Jeff reached into a bag, saying, "Dale, we have a cap for you too."

The cap bore a Washington State logo on the front of it and I slipped it on my head. It provided for a great photo opportunity. Then Jeff handed me a cooler filled, not with bone marrow, but with fresh salmon fillets from Pike Place Fish Market.

If you happened to be an outsider at the airport that day, you would have probably thought long-separated brothers were being reunited. Nancy, Courtney, Emily, and I tried to show in every smile, handshake, and hug our deep gratitude for Jeff's actions the previous December. Jeff and Krista were trying to figure out what this all meant; to be here in Abilene, meeting my family and me, and sharing our story.

We loaded up their luggage and headed to our house so our new friend and his family could unpack and settle in for the full weekend. Our plans for the night included dinner at a restaurant, after which we would return home to prepare for a busy Friday, which included Jeff's parents and sister arriving from Arizona.

The next morning, Jeff and I left the house early to do a radio spot with Rudy Fernandez and KEAN radio to promote the health fair. After we completed the radio spot, we finished some last-minute tasks for the health fair the next day. Everywhere we went my friends took the time to express their appreciation to Jeff for his willingness to donate bone marrow to save my life. I intentionally avoided those who might have said, "What on earth did you save Dale for?"

Nancy, Krista, and the girls met up with us later to visit Frontier Texas, a museum dedicated to the old settler days in our state's history. After touring the museum, Jeff's parents and sister joined us for dinner at Perini's, a famous steakhouse in Buffalo Gap. Jeff wasn't much of a fish eater, so I wanted him to have the best Texas grilled steak possible. From the looks of his plate, he left satisfied.

The next morning Jeff and I drove to Pioneer Drive to set up for the health fair. Many friends and family came to help with this special day. Phil and Courtney set up Callie's Lemonade-for-a-Cure Stand under oak trees near the church's entrance, where they enjoyed a steady stream of visitors. Every dollar given for a glass of lemonade went to assist the Make-a-Wish Foundation in their efforts to fulfill an ill child's dream.

Inside the cafeteria, visitors registered with Be-The-Match to be bone marrow donors, agreed to be organ donors, and learned more about our Hope and Help ministry to cancer patients. Those interested in donating blood walked across the hall to a room set up with several stations. After visiting the various booths, those making life-changing commitments enjoyed breakfast or lunch, depending on when they arrived at the health fair.

The health fair provided an opportunity to tell our story and potentially save lives. Since the registration event, I know Be-The-Match has contacted at least one person registered that day to donate bone marrow for a transplant that will hopefully give new life to the recipient. I also know that the health fair set a Meek Blood Center record for donated blood. Jeff and I drove to my home that Saturday afternoon elated over the day's successes.

After a good night's sleep, which we all needed after a long but productive day, we left the house and drove the short distance to church for worship. Our pastor preached a message that day that made clear that the blood of Christ atones for our sins, and that we become children of God through His sacrifice.

After church we wanted to enjoy our remaining time together. We drove around to show the girls our horse and let them see the small ranch land Jerry and I own. Nancy and the girls rode in one car, and Jeff and I rode in my pickup. The Sunday afternoon drive gave Jeff and me time to share how we came to faith in Christ, our dreams for our families, and my desire to keep collaborating in order to save lives as he had saved mine.

On Monday afternoon, Nancy and I escorted our new friends to the airport. We were all fatigued and emotionally spent from the weekend but rejoicing in what the Lord had brought together. We walked with Jeff and his family to the security checkpoint and said our good-byes. I hugged Jeff and shared with him the words Brother Abraham had said to me a decade earlier: "If I don't see you again, I'll see you in Heaven."

* * * *

One of the most visited rivers in Texas is the Frio River. It runs through Garner State Park in Uvalde County. It's a cool, clear river with a luminous surface reflecting towering Cypress trees. The Frio is so popular with Texans that it appears in the lyrics of a George Strait country tune.

When Courtney was ten, Emily eight, and Malory three, our family joined Keith, Lorraine, and my parents at this popular summer destination in Texas. Rivers in south Texas were renowned for river tubing – you just grabbed a tube and floated along on the current at a gentle pace, though the current occasionally sped up.

We left our then toddler, Malory, with my parents after lunch and took off to float the river. Keith and I floated in tubes, while Nancy, Lorraine, and my two daughters sat in a raft paddling down the river. The raft held the beach towels and cooler of food.

We reached a fork in the river where a sign indicated rafters had to take one fork and tubers the other. I had to untie the rope that connected my brother-in-law and me to the girls. We told our wives we would meet them downriver.

Keith and I floated along in shallow water we could stand in, while the girls went to a deeper fork that headed toward a small but treacherous waterfall. We failed to see any posted warning of the approaching danger. As I floated down the parallel fork, I spotted the girls as they approached the waterfall. The raft dipped. Emily and Lorraine flew off and were forced down river. I couldn't see Nancy and Courtney, but I knew they were in trouble when Lorraine yelled, "Keith! Dale Richard!"

We jumped out of our tubes and ran across the river rocks in waist-high water. When we reached the shore we headed straight towards Courtney and Nancy. Lorraine had Emily as the current pulled them downstream, but the undertow had pulled Courtney and Nancy under the water. It tugged at them, making it impossible to swim away from the waterfall's base. To complicate matters, the rope that had connected our tubes to the raft had wrapped around Nancy's leg. Courtney and Nancy popped up within the churning water at the base of the falls only to get sucked under again like a bobber pulled by a fish. This happened twice, and I prayed they would come up a third time.

Fifty yards away from Nancy and Courtney, I found it impossible to swim upstream as the current slammed me against a boulder in the water and busted my lip. I raised my head out of the water and glimpsed two young men standing on the bank watching Courtney and Nancy. I had noticed them sitting on the bank before we were separated from the girls. My next quick glance saw the two men standing in the fierce current. One of the young men waded against the water's pull and went under, grabbed Courtney, and was able to kick out towards the shoreline. The second rescuer managed to free Nancy's leg from the rope and tow her to safety. I saw the men carry Nancy and Courtney to the bank seemingly without difficulty. Once on shore they checked to make sure Nancy and Courtney were okay, and then they disappeared.

Keith helped Lorraine and Emily to shore, while I made sure Nancy and Courtney were fine. Other than being out of breath and ghostly pale from fear, the girls would recover. I looked around to find the men to thank them for saving my wife and daughter. A small crowd had gathered around my family. I asked, "Do any of you see where those young men went? Do you know anything about them?" No one had any idea who the men were or where they went.

It all seemed rather mysterious, but I knew without a doubt that those strong young men prevented certain disaster. They were in the right place at the right time. Were they angels? Were they regular people? My family fully believes they stood in the water as angelic lifeguards sent from God. You could never convince anyone present that those two young men weren't God's guardian angels.

* * * *

What does it mean that Jeff went to the hospital to donate blood, and years later received a call to donate his bone marrow? How significant is it that he endured the pain required to access his bone marrow? It means he jumped in to save a life of someone he didn't know. It may not have required the same bravery or risk, but it achieved the same result. Had I not received a bone marrow transplant from a man with antibodies to the JC virus, I can't say with any degree of certainty that I would be alive today. To say I am grateful is to scratch only the surface of my appreciation. God sent a man to rescue me. Jeff is my hero. Jeff is my lifeguard. This time, our rescuer didn't remain mysteriously unknown. The Lord allowed him to become my friend.

CONCLUSION

WITHOUT HIM

Without God's miraculous intervention in my life, I wouldn't have stayed alive on more than one occasion. With every physical challenge, I faced a test of my resolve to live. I am thankful to have passed those tests to this point in life. Those victories gave Nancy and me additional opportunities to witness more miracles together. God's providence has permitted me to see Callie grow to be a completely healthy, cancer-free six-year-old who started kindergarten this past August. I've also had the privilege of sitting in the waiting room as three more grandchildren entered the world: Andrew, Natalie, and Corley. Our ninth grandchild, Brooklyn, is due in the fall of 2015. The Lord has blessed my family.

Without God's healing of my heart, I would be dead for eternity. With Christ as my Savior, Jesus has promised me an abundant life now and a dwelling for eternity with my Heavenly Father – a promise he makes to all children of God.

There is no way I can keep such good news to myself. Today, I work diligently to share the good news of Jesus Christ. Chuck Reynolds, pastor of Grace Baptist Church in Potosi, and I lead a monthly men's meeting at a local restaurant to challenge men to grow in their faith. Every month new men come to this meeting. Some men are attorneys and businessmen. Others are laborers. Some are searching for answers, while others have known Christ for years.

Nancy and I continue to hear from concerned friends and family members of people with cancer. Almost daily, my phone rings with a request to make a visit. We fulfill as many requests as we can, and, with each one, the gospel is the most important part of my conversation. I want every cancer patient – every person for that matter – to have the assurance of salvation. I am thankful the Lord saved me as a young child and that the difficult situations of my life can now bring new acquaintances and old friends to faith in Jesus Christ.

My Quotes and Sayings

You gotta want it.

We work hard and then we play hard. There is time for both, but it's done in that order.

Look a person in the eyes when you speak.

Let your yes be yes and your no be no. Don't ride the fence.

You can catch more bees with honey than vinegar.

A dollar waiting on a nickel, you have ninety-five cents to catch up with me.

Don't loan money out you can't lose, but give and don't ask for it back. It's a gift.

A fool and his money will soon part company.

Make a hand, or lend a hand, but don't stand.

You're not at work to get hours. You're at work to make your boss a profit. In that way, you will have all the hours you want or need.

Never be anywhere that you don't want Jesus to see you.

Set priorities. God first, family second, work third.

Put a smile on your face, and if you can't smile, fake it till you can.

Finish better than you started.

Quitters never win, and winners never quit.

Listen twice as much as you speak.

Be the first one to the job.

Give your children a little slack but be quick to pull back.

Go wash your face off.

Conversation is like baseball. Both persons have to catch the ball and throw it back.

You must be friendly to have friends.

Let little ones win, so they will play with you again.

If you have to win all the time, you're a loser.

Work hard or go home.

A little kindness goes a long way.

It takes 100 kind words to cover up one harsh word.

We aren't able to forget but we must forgive.

Without faith in Christ, there is no hope.

Without hope, there is no victory.

Every unbeliever has a void in his or her life.

Brother Abraham Bhasme greeting Jay Capra and me in Bangalore, Karnataka.

My mother, Delores Morrison, and I visit in her hospital room.

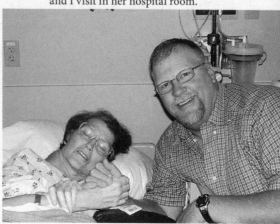

My family gathered to celebrate a family tradition. The first one to the Kemp city limit sign won a candy bar. Pictured are Nancy, me, Phil, Malory, Courtney, Dad, Garin, Corby, Lorraine, Emily, and Caleb.

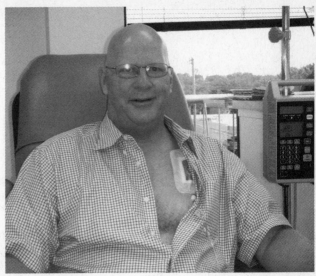

Receiving chemotherapy treatment.

Leaning against the "pregnant" tree at the Malakoff farm.

Football.

A cool look from high school.

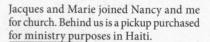
Jacques and Marie joined Nancy and me for church. Behind us is a pickup purchased for ministry purposes in Haiti.

Brother Abraham sitting with Malory in our home.

A police officer in Port-au-Prince gave me a picture to remember his daughter who died from injuries sustained in the earthquake.

Nancy, Carson, Callie, and me.

Ben Gray stands with a lady testing out the water from a Global Samaritan water purification system.

Church rubble from the Haiti earthquake.

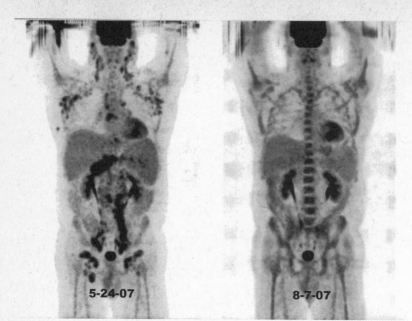

Before- and after-treatment PET scans in May 2007.

Scan showing the virus on my brain in October 2010.

Scan of my brain that showed the decrease of the virus by February 2011.

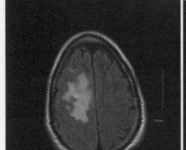

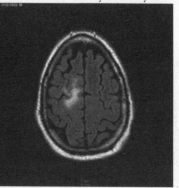

Contents of the Hope and Help bags.

Nancy and I on South Padre Island, May 2011.

Walking Malory down the aisle at Logsdon Chapel on her wedding day, March 5, 2011.

Callie after the surgery to remove her brain tumor, June 2011.

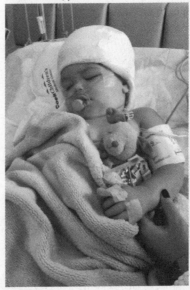

Nancy on Malory's wedding day.

Carson, my grandson, shaved his head to show his support during chemo.

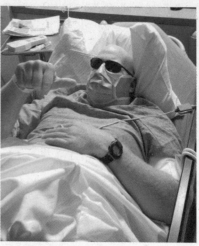

Resting in the hospital room two weeks before the BMT.

Transplant day!

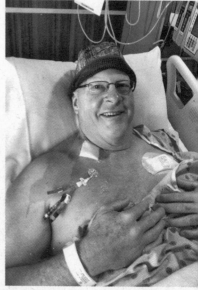

Preparing for the bone marrow transplant, December 2012.

A view standing on the tank dam looking towards the lake house.

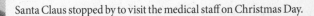

I am holding Jeff
Babbitt's bone marrow.

Santa Claus stopped by to visit the medical staff on Christmas Day.

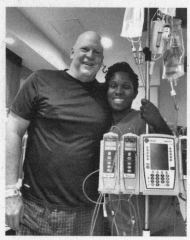

A nurse and I say hello on the BMT floor.

Callie and I take a picture to promote the health fair with Jeff Babbitt and Callie's lemonade stand.

Our grandchildren: Ryan, Carson holding Andrew, Natalie, Corley Ellie, Callie with Addison in front of her.

Nancy and I wait for the brain biopsy. It took everything I had to smile and give a thumbs up.

Nancy and I celebrating Malory's wedding day.

Nancy and I on New Year's Eve 2012, a week after my transplant. Hard to have a New Year's kiss while wearing the masks.

Grandkids on July 4. Back row: Ryan, Ellie, Addison, Callie, Carson. Front row: Natalie, Corley, Andrew.

Picture with Jeff Babbitt at a restaurant in Abilene.

The one-year celebration of my transplant. Back row: Steve, Phil, and Courtney.
Front row: Malory, Nancy, me, Emily, and Jacob.